DESGRACIADO

ANGEL DOMINGUEZ

DESGRACIADO

THE COLLECTED LETTERS

NIGHTBOAT BOOKS
NEW YORK

ISBN: 978-1-64362-114-2

COVER ART, "DESGRACIADO" BY THE AUTHOR
DESIGN AND TYPESETTING BY KIT SCHLUTER

CATALOGING-IN-PUBLICATION DATA IS AVAILABLE FROM
THE LIBRARY OF CONGRESS

NIGHTBOAT BOOKS
NEW YORK
WWW.NIGHTBOAT.ORG

For all kin

FROM OUR SHARED DISGRACE

FOREWORD BY RAQUEL SALAS RIVERA

> *Y nadie pregunta*
> *si sufro, si lloro,*
> *si tengo una pena*
> *que hiere muy hondo.*
>
> *And no one asks*
> *if I suffer, if I cry,*
> *if I have a sorrow*
> *that pains me deep inside.*

"EL CANTANTE," HÉCTOR LAVOE

MY FRIEND MONA RECENTLY ASKED ME WHAT I NEEDED HER TO bring me when she visited Puerto Rico. Her wording, like many of the things we say to those we love, betrayed a contraband truth: "What do you need from the US?" I smiled. How to answer such a question?! It was loaded with the seemingly contradictory relations that make up the entangled mess of our particular brand of colonialism, one in which our archipelago remains bound to the most powerful empire in the most predictable of ways. For what *did* I need from the US? I soon came up with two responses. The first was that I, that we, need nothing. The second: that we need freedom. How can we simultaneously need both nothing and freedom from that constellation of borders, companies, and nationalized privatizations?

To need *from* is, in many ways, a contract. One needs something another possesses, but also that another has the power to give. If I were to say, "I need your toy," you would cease to exist as a subject, except to indicate an interruption between myself and the toy. You would exist solely as the possessor of the object, and I would exist solely as a subject that is unfulfilled in their desire for possession. But if I were to say, "I need the toy from you," my words would bring agency into both of us. You would become someone capable of giving, and I of requesting and possibly receiving. This would make it an unsigned contract: an acknowledgment of present ownership and a request for exchange. Although presented as a statement, it would also be haunted by the open-endedness that characterizes questions, one that accompanies all stated desires.

If I state that I need rest, and direct myself to a room full of friends that includes my lover, I may want my lover to hear the request in my statement. Now, if I state to my partner that I need to rest from our relationship (now we are, of course, alone), it is more confusing. Am I avoiding saying I want to end things for fear of causing harm or am I hoping they will hear the request for change, despite my bluntness, and take my need to be an indication that there is still space for me to need *from* them? In other words, do I need something they can actually give?

Then there is another problem, that of possession and the fulfilment of desire. See, when we need something and another possesses it, we say we need it *from* them. But *from* also implies origin in a way that is eclipsed by the conditional temporality of the exchange. We need from them because right now they happen to have it. Yet if I say I need something from you, and that something is love, or that something is freedom, then it is something you might hold for now, but something that cannot belong to you the way a toy belongs to a child.

I return to the question of our freedom from the country that has colonized us, that has sustained that colonial relationship, and that continues to colonize, through both maintenance and displacement. The question of our freedom *from* is different and the same as the question of our *freedom*. It is this word *from* that somehow suspends a singular exchange, like a dead star shining out into our future. This word makes it seem as if empire is both the origin and guardian of freedom, both its source and owner. In capitalism's obsession with the present, Marx once saw a denial of its inevitable demise. Like a relationship that has long outrun its course, *from* lets us cling to the dead star possibility that our partner will change into what we need. It is a statement we are afraid to transform into a question (Will you give me freedom?) or a demand (Give me freedom!), and thus remains a wishful thought we didn't mean to say out loud.

For freedom can only be given when it has been taken, and it can only be taken back. It comes into being when neither giving nor taking have occupied our lives. It is the absence of itself, in that we only know it and speak it because we know or have known unfreedom, and we only fully live it when no one can come and claim it. This *from* erases a concept of freedom that precedes ownership and that, despite its totalizing efforts, capitalism never truly abolishes: the freedom empire is holding hostage never belonged to anyone. Our freedom does not belong to us anymore than we belong to our existence. And thus, for now, we need freedom *from* the us, in that it has trapped what will one day be released, but we do not need a freedom originating in the us (from the us). Most importantly, we don't need a freedom that is given, but rather our freedom, the freedom that is there within us, that has been taken only in the brevity of exchange, and that will find its way back to us as we have often found our way back home drunk and high, wondering the next day: *how the fuck did I make it?* Because our feet remember freedom, its dips, turns, and dead ends.

As I write this, colonialism is inventing new ways of taking that freedom hostage. The latest wave of colonization has brought Logan Paul to Puerto Rico with a whole crew of colonizer bros searching for paradise in a pandemic. My cousin, his partner, and I head to the Cabo Rojo Guaniquilla National Wildlife Reserve, and discover a strip of private land now cuts through the public reserve in such a way that the beaches have become inaccessible to the "public." When we ask the private security guard if the sea is also private, he smirks and answers, "No, of course not." Yet, as he says this, he is closing the giant blue gate that limits us to a designated loop. We are being sold privately and, when we try to go to the places we have loved our entire lives, we find our ecosystems have been taken over by investors, venture capitalists, sold-out politicians, and anyone else with the capital to steal without consequence.

As I write this, I am wrapping up two semesters of teaching Angel Dominguez's *Desgraciado* to students at the University of Puerto Rico, a public institution that is being dismantled and privatized by the Junta, the oligarchical Oversight and Management Board established by the PROMESA law to implement neoliberal policies and budget cuts to education, health care, housing, and all the services that help Puerto Ricans survive. My students loved the book because they saw themselves in the poet's tortured relationship with his colonizer and the never-ending colonial past. When Angel's face popped up on their screen during a class visit, they began asking them an array of questions about what it felt like to finally be able to speak back, even if only to the mirage, to their colonizer.

In recent years, we have witnessed an obsession with the monumentality of statues. Back in 2017, the white supremacist "Unite the Right" rally in Charlottesville, Virginia, which resulted in the death of an activist and the national visibility of an emboldened right, was organized in response to the proposal that the Confederate Robert E. Lee statue be removed. During the period leading up to the summer protests of 2020, across the United States organizations and individuals asked that other statutes be eliminated or replaced, and for the nation to reexamine what is deemed worthy of glorification and what is considered shameful about an imagined collective history. It is in this context that I, a Puerto Rican who is not and will never be a US American, have repeatedly returned to Dominguez's book, which offers us a tearing down or disgracing of the colonizer's statue, accompanied by a living record of the messiness colonialism leaves in its wake.

Originally published as a chapbook for Econo Textual Objects, *Desgraciado* can best be described as an involucramiento with sixteenth century Spanish murderer, pillager, and rapist Fray Diego de Landa. The word "involucrar," originating from the Latin "involūcrum," translates as envelope, encasing, or covering. To be involucradx is to be more than involved. A person who is involucradx is enveloped by and entangled with that with which they are involved. Footage of anti-fascists and fascists at protests shows them knotted in kicks, stabs, and beatings. Similarly, the violence in Dominguez and de Landa's involucramiento is a Benjaminian monad, a determining moment into which the past, present, and future collapse. It is this involucramiento that had me reading *Desgraciado* out loud with my friend Farid, both of us in tears, remembering that we have never been alone.

The word "desgraciado" literally means he/she/they that have fallen out of God's grace, to be disgraced. Colloquially, however, to be a "desgraciado" is to be despicable. *¡Eres un desgraciado!* was a terrible insult for my grandmother's generation; it meant you were the worst of the worst, and not even God could save you. The letters in this book cut across genres. They could be read as poems, letters, prose poems, seances, curses, prayers, "spirit balm[s]; […] elixir[s]; […] riot[s]; [or…] form[s] of living." Sometimes, Dominguez is the desgraciado, "A D(og)" thrown out on the street, un "animal[…] del monte salvaje," outside of God's grace before God could even arrive to colonize his people. Sometimes, de Landa is the desgraciado, caught in history as the colonizer's ghost, forever cursed by those he burned. Sometimes, they are both desgraciados, involucradxs in a history that must be remembered, must be invoked, if we are to change this world.

Throughout *Desgraciado*, Dominguez writes one-way letters, whispering secrets to a dead man so we may overhear. When I first read this collection back in 2016, I immediately recalled Jack Spicer's *After Lorca*, a book where Spicer invokes Federico García Lorca as a dead and unrequited lover, much like Dominguez invokes the Spanish colonizer Diego de Landa. Yet, unlike Spicer, Dominguez seems to be sustaining the relationship only in order to wound back. These entangled forms of struggle (correspondence, translation, caretaking, poison) unfold within relations of duress that have lasted centuries, almost turning these letters into vengeance by correspondence. They mirror the proximity of colonial violence in these involucramientos, and yet they do so in order that we may dream beyond the relationship between de Landa and the poet. Through these writings, the colonized tries to free themself the colonizer, but the correspondence reminds us that colonial structures play out in intimacy precisely because those scenes are repeating themselves elsewhere in both public and private spheres. By openly bringing genocide into the bedroom, and the bedroom into the colonizer's history, Dominguez changes the game.

I have never read a book like *Desgraciado*. Ok, maybe César Vallejo's *Trilce*. Okkkkkk maybe Federico García Lorca's *Poeta en Nueva York*. Fine, Anjelamaría Dávila's *Animal fiero y tierno*. What I'm saying is, it is that good. So, when Angel Dominguez asked for a foreword, I myself became involucradx: fear, rejection, love, devotion, all those things condensed into the word "yes." I felt this because there is a compañerismo in our own exchanges I hope to always honor through our writing.

We need each other and we need each other's words. We need freedom the way we need each other, the way we need love. It is a need that only understands its fulfillment or loss. Those who oppress us will never fulfill us. That is why this book is a book about desire, because the desire for freedom structures colonial relations, and the impossibility of its fulfillment drives colonial production. Dominguez has always understood this. Perhaps because they are a Scorpio, or perhaps because it has guided their life, this seeking, in a way that cuts through the bullshit dreamscape of the world's Diego de Landas. By writing *Desgraciado*, a book that looks straight at the mess they left behind and the fire they keep stoking, Angel Dominguez/Ángel Domínguez/A D(og), already sato y realengo, has written the colonizer and the colonized out of language. Here, the erasures of colonization speak a language of silences that shatters the breaths we take between signs, which is why, so often while reading these letters, I must remind myself to breathe. May their words guide you back to yourself, as they have guided me time and time again, and may you read Dominguez's poems in your solitudes, your losses, and your futures.

SANTURCE, PUERTO RICO, 2021

DESGRACIADO

Dear Diego,

did i ever tell you i too line betwixt two streams
when it rains? i smile at these small similarities
in a bashful shame of having written you love letters
for all these years. what are we to one another?
Would you care if you knew i was writing to you all these
years later? 455 years is a long time. Long enough to
see the oppressor's empire fall. Long enough to see
every one of the so called explorers, dead. What
am i become to myself? Who am i all these years
later? Tato's mother calls it Colonial sickness.
    The latent radiation poisoning that is colonization.

God bless the rage in us.
It's how we know each other.

TERRANCE HAYES, *Wind in a Box*

…it was in the year 62, on the part of the Franciscan religious, who had taken us to teach the doctrine, instead of which they began to torment us, hanging us by the hands and whipping us cruelly, hanging weights of stone on our feet, torturing many of us on a windlass, giving the torture of the water, from which many died or were maimed… May fray Diego de Landa and his companions suffer the penance for the evils they have done to us, and may our descendants to the forth generation be recompensed the great persecution that came on us.

LETTER TO THE KING OF SPAIN, APRIL 12, 1567

SIGNED BY:
DON FRANCISCO DE MONTEJO XIU, GOV. OF MANI
JUAN PACAB, GOV. OF MUNA
JORGE XIU, GOV. OF PANABÁ
FRANCISCO PACAB, GOV. OF TE-XUL

TRANSLATED BY WILLIAM GATES

Diego,

The world is bigger than we will ever know.

Diego—you dead man—I write to you.

It's been centuries, I'm sure, since someone called out to you; now I do: Diego de Landa. The year is 2014 and the calendar's been reset—your story buried beneath yr auto-de-fé burning our bodies down—we've no one to rescue that sound. But what am I saying? I speak English into robots and write to you in anything but Spanish—lengua Catalan—I wanted you to know, I've touched your soil and throughout Madrid and Barcelona I carved large red letters in churches and chapels, painted "MAYAN CONQUEST" on subways and buses, wrote "FUCK SPAIN" over every flag I could find. I started small fires in museums and stopped short of smashing mirrors and windows; I can't erase you now—there's too much to wipe out on data disks and clouds—fire couldn't find you now—perhaps you'll drown—I'll pull you through dzonots on my gringo tongue—rinse your lungs clean with Xibalba water—what would you say to me then, and could your heart be pure?—I'd have to taste test the ash of your organs & fiddle with your bones to be certain I could trust you to go on dying, un-acquitted by the light of time, I want your trial to continue; maybe I want to save you.

Love,
A

Dear Diego,

The skies are full of dragonflies today and everyone fetishizes my name. I'm reminded of this when engaging with the institution. Is it Angel or Ángel? I always say: whatever you find easiest to pronounce. But really I'd prefer no name or pronoun; it's these instances of being acutely aware of my "race" that bring me back to you. Or you back to me, I'm not sure which it is. If it is. If I keep thinking of writing these letters, will I ever get our lungs alight. I can't make a fire. I'm trying to yield more than I advance. I am learning that not all words are always heard or spoken, though in this moment I hope every dictionary snaps its spine into a deafening ocean. Diego, I worry about things like Spanish proficiency tests for dual-citizenship, PhD programs, and the accumulated suffering brought on by "globalization." I remember learning about manifest destiny in my Cortez middle school whose mascot was a conquistador. I remember getting angry every time we watched a national geographic documentary about the benefits of imperialism. Benefits like my bastardized name. LAUSD Chalupa Tuesdays. A colonizer on every corner. I wonder what they would have called me if your language never came. Between you and me, I really prefer the name Chaac.

Love,
Rain.

Dear Diego,

Do you know what it's like to live as a ghost? Was this your experience in returning to Spain to stand trial? To walk familiar streets, recognizing things: how they've changed; how they stayed the same. What was it then to even travel between continents—or months on end, stuck with your own thoughts. I'm sure you worked out your defense carefully. I read an online article by an expat (white man) who referred to your auto-defé as a "bonfire." I looked up the definition of the word, because I couldn't believe its place within the context of your crime. I found this: bonfire | bän͵fī(-ə)r noun. A large open-air fire used as part of a celebration, for burning trash, or as a signal. ORIGIN late Middle English: from bone + fire. The term originally denoted a large open-air fire on which bones were burned (sometimes as part of a celebration), also one for burning heretics or proscribed literature. Dr. Johnson accepted the mistaken idea that the word came from the French bon "good." I don't know what else to say. I forgot why I was writing this letter. I guess I just needed someone to talk to. I've pined for the face of the colonizer in place of my own, or perhaps severed and placed upon my outline. The idea of this book burns a hole through my abdomen; I can't quite shake the quiet of my ancestry. A lack left behind by the magic of globalism. Give up a tongue to take another, and so now I write to you in English.

A

Dear Diego,

Do you know what it means to go home? Have you ever felt that safety—the calm that comes with sleep? Do you know what it's like to sleep, to dream? Do you still dream? It seems I've got a lot of questions for you these days; your silence a constant Kōan. I don't know how to talk to you, though I do most every day. Or rather, I think of you until I have to write to you and I realize that I never really write: you. It's always this approximation that lacks a temperament. You lack a temperature. You lack a sense of woe. Sometimes, I fold you up into an idea. Sometimes, I let myself eat what's left of you. I pine for the you in me. I pine for control of time. Or history. Which matters more? Did you know that Latinx/Xicanx people are over 51% of Los Angeles now? Soon to be the "majority" in this country. I wonder if we'll reset the ledger then. I wonder if that's when history can become undone. Diego, did I ever tell you I was placed into ESL because of my last name? It wasn't until I couldn't do my homework in Spanish (somewhere around the third assignment) that I brought it up to my mother, who was furious; I was ashamed I couldn't finish my work in Spanish. We weren't supposed to speak Spanish outside of my grandparent's house. It felt like I still should have been able to. It still feels like I should be able to. But I can't. It wasn't until years later that I learned Los Angeles public schools receive extra funding for every ESL/bilingual student they enroll; I never saw a cent of this money; the exploitation of Brown bodies within the white institution is all too familiar. How many ways must I ask my oppressor to pronounce me properly? How much more evidence of western intelligence must I accumulate? I am so sick of morphing my body and becoming unfamiliar to myself. I keep explaining myself to others as dog. An outside dog. Scraggly city coyote, not made for the white institutions or their structures; I am many and cannot be contained; I can't come inside the house because I found a Brown radiance strong enough to end the drought of my spirit. I found that we were never meant to be in the house porque somos lluvia.

Love,
CHAAC

Dear Diego,

I wake up this morning and see "Where did the ancient Maya disappear to, and why?" (as if we're not still here); "sacred Mayan sex positions involving a hammock" (think of how you've fucked us into this fetishized obscurity of a vanished people)—"too many people spend time thinking about the Mayan's 2012 predictions and not enough time thinking of their tantric sex powers."

I couldn't make this shit up.

I listen to white narrators describe the "curse" of the Maya as these güerros dive into our portals. I listen to myself say "our" like I've lived there longer than a few trips, I'm just as misplaced as they may be. Sifting through dictionaries and encyclopedias, resisting Big Pharma and the temptation of artisan DNA tests, I bet they profit off our spit somehow. Gathering our genes; spitting colonies into our mouths with their all important pop-up ads evacuating our dreams. Convincing us and the general public that we are just vanished aliens. Oddities from the colonial imaginary. Yet here I am, trying to remember what came before you, dead man. Trying to remember the color of my mother's mother's mother's mother's mother's mother's eyes. The shape of our nose. The sound of the spit that spoke non-Spanish stories into memory. What were we before all this language arrived?

-A(nother)

Dear Diego,

I write to you in a distant tongue. When I speak Spanish, I feel like I'm trying on shorts I know won't fit. They might button up, but I muffin top, and I'm painfully aware. I slip on English like a nighty; I'm comfortable when it's loose, it breathes with my body. It doesn't hurt me, at least not always. Diego, the present continues and I imagine the fabric of English upon my body—what would be its print? I guess I'd say the fabric would be blood-drenched cotton, the cut would be short, mid-thigh, I see a flower print, but I want the color to be blood before it dries. A shy sheen. It's intimate but I wear it often. I never take it off really. Crumpling up the smallest bits of myself into its pockets; rewriting those bits until I'm convinced I'm over-writing and trying so desperately to disappear. I guess I'll write again if the writing happens.

Love,
A

Diego,

I want to tell you of how I have been hugging myself, crouching in the shower for years—I heard my mother crying in a midnight once, and once I was a river or was in a river and found the memory of a mother-mourning into a sopping red rag, it covered my face and took the sun away. Diego, do you remember why it was you did as you did? Was the purpose of fire to reiterate a Catholic hell? By tossing our bodies to the fire you made death something it is not. You. And yet I, too, am complicit (my robot wanted to write complicated) in colonization, from where I find these words in time, entrenched within a system of systems that continuously shrouds itself as "brave," yet bloated in the face—grease of slaughtered pigs upon the mouth, the pigs and their babies. I write this while, of course, thinking of tacos from Los Angeles, a beautifully turbid smog encrusted shimmering rattlesnake-bird of a place. See, I grew up without this language. Without access to language. That wasn't important. What was important was making it in this capitalist society, to be inside the house, even if on your knees, and not beside it at the window. Looking in. I picked a path of breaking and entering, harmless thefts of education, experiences of time loss and alcohol. "There you go talking white again," he would always say, just to get a rise out of me—whiteness here being equated with intelligence, which despite its "usefulness" in regards to American socioeconomic mobility was also a danger. It was this white tongue after all that took all our stories. Was there a trickle of ash upon your lips left I might lick off? I want to lick it off—show you dog memory, resist the urge to become violent. I want you dead in another way. Maybe I can save you.

Dear Diego,

My position was "dissolved" today, a week after surviving a near fatal car accident. I decided to leave the office early because, really, who gives a fuck anymore? I was unable to conform or be institutionalized; I called these virtue signaling phonies on their bullshit and I don't feel bad for what I've done. I feel bad for all I've ever done. I feel bad for not being more than what I am right now. I called my grandmother to apologize for leaving. Voyaging out into the whiteness of the world in search of my own name. Trying to find a resemblance in the mouths of my oppressors. I'm sitting in a Bank waiting on a faceless figure to tell me what I already know, and it makes me wonder: what did you know of debt? I mean, you were a friar; I don't know what you are now. Did you know that, after you died, your country went bankrupt; all the gold and culture you stole was for naught. It didn't matter—we all wound up poor, some of us more impoverished than others. We lost part of our tongue and grew yours in our mouths. We swapped vital organs and spirit fluids. Fuck it, I'm not even going to mail this one out.

Dear Diego,

I keep trying to write the same thing down. The sleeping never really arrives so much as vanishes and that constant struggle of time tumbles over onto itself; these sentences are music. I get dizzy and drunk off that sound. But I've already written that now. And now I'm onto something new. Something I haven't/didn't think I could do. But there I go again getting swayed by those sounds; they're all a bit removed, leaning heavy on their vowels. But what do you do with that. When you're too head in the flowers to know how to communicate that awful howling blue that stinks of dissociation and daylight? It's a long time before I can really process anything enough to ever write anything down. This is me, failing. I don't care if I fail. I suppose now I am dreaming without fear of waking—charging forward into that unknown dissonant sound that creates a seed pod memory—that blank eucalyptus that blossoms honey flowers in the form of butterflies. It takes a lot to get me to write anything down these days. So busy thinking. Too busy absorbing the everything that consumes me. I say, I try to write it down but really I don't; I slow down to observe, remember, and rearrange my tongue. Rarely does the sentence occur. At least not outside my own skull. The rumble never gets out; the tremor mellows out into a steady curl; the wave never breaks. It's always sunset where I come from, always a matter of seeing.

Dreaming,
A

Dear Diego,

Can I tell you something? I've never been good at Spanish. All my friends expect this tongue from me; they say: lick it: lick the space of language between us. Sometimes, I expect it too. And then I get there, and I remember how I never learned Spanish. At least not formally, in a school. And it makes me crazy. I should know more than I know, shouldn't I? And then there's all this guilt. The body I've buried beside myself; inside myself—it retches for hours—I can't even keep water down. This body vomits the sun. Diego—there is too much to tell you. How do I start? How did you start? What was that even— to infect a foreign (land) body with such confidence—you've got the word of god, that thistle lisping tongue that sounds wrong to me, like it robbed our land, our bodies blind of themselves. Now I can't tell what I am. Cog, dog, prey, poem, bastard, bitch. My blood blooms hot tracts of earth that shatter when I think of becoming, or what I have become. I think of you more than I'd like to admit. I work out a poem, or rather, I've been planning on writing a poem called: "I see my biological father several times a day." Sometimes, I really think I'll write the poem. Just like I think I'll write this book. Just like I think I might find him. Sometimes, I think it's you. I imagine your absent image. Sunlight-circle denoting a sense of "holy" or #Blessed. Diego, I think we have to dance. I need you in my bed to understand you. I house you in my body. I lick the language between us; spit up blood. My mouth tastes like pennies in a desert. Your heart tastes like a mouthful of cocaine. I can't swallow. I vomit bombs over Dresden. I vomit lost notebooks into the archives of my oppressor. I (un)write your book. Diego, you lie down on a bed of flowers, and I'll drag your body across Sunset Blvd., from Figueroa to the beach. Obliteration and bliss are synonymous. If I threw you into the fire would you burn? Auto-de-fé—act-of-faith—a—Fire. A fire. A fire between us.

Love,
A D(og)

Dear,

The plume of smoke was hidden from history by night. What sleeps in the violence we don't address? We're in the basement now. I skip sentences across dreams, or skip dreams across the length of my blood. Why do I keep eating my crystals and poems while dreaming? Dreaming of becoming crystal body remnant/artifact/left over. An accidental relic. I am not a relic—but writing, isn't that how you found me? Wasn't it writing that was so threatening—that needed to be destroyed—does this language live in me, the language of absence? I'm a never, floating up there through the centuries into new sleeps of pen and breath, coughing asthmatic—eyes red from your holy smokes and before we smoke, I wrote how much I actually love the color of your eyes in mine, amor.

Dear Diego,

We, los animales del monte salvaje, have nothing to fear when they've already taken everything from us. They wanted death to be punishment, to be permanent, and yet these charred bodies push themselves out of the earth—art of the earth pushes itself out of the night to form a terrain in the form of rain—this rain—it is raining right now to extinguish the fire of history. The history of 56 million ancestors erased and executed. Enough ancestors to affect the climate of the planet. Setting fire to the master's house. I'm still locked inside the language; it is still on fire; these atrocities just won't die. I'm still burning with revenge. Won't you sniff my flesh, or press a paw to raw body? I want you to chip off the charcoal. Even where it sticks. Let me see me before the politicized body; let me reach into mine own cage before biting into blood, tongues, heart & hands—wild-eyed with lungs full of gods you'd rather not fuck with. Give my body back to animals. Fuck a colonial casket. My organs are for the land that bore me. Rub my kidneys into the asphalt streets; let my liver sleep in a neon pit; draw a line of blood around the crossroads of my living—strip flesh as needed—tear with teeth.

Dear Diego,

How could we treat your words as your own, fire vulture? You've no proof of your being—no more than I mine. You murdered us to bring forth the second coming of Jesus, and he came bukkake style.

He came in the form of plastic rosaries and swap meet tilmas y velas. He came spreading his empire of wax and sand in exchange for gold—we didn't want gold—didn't want this old tongue, rough as jaguar pelt brushing up against a plot of graves. He came with 3D televisions and high-definition speakers and twenty-five cent electric prayers. He came without ever coming; not even those teachings, on the backs of three hundred cattle were from his absent hand. Not even coming to help with the citizenship tests, letting the paperwork eat the people, only to end up missing; palms outstretched cupping the flag of their oppressors from afar. A litany of ghost teeth whistling across the land.

The record does not exist, and yet the language of burial persists in forgetting what's happened; no one told me. I felt it in my body. I remembered: fire. I could not see through your obsidian heart to reach the other side, over four hundred and fifty years later, I still want you with me. We keep each other safe.

Dear Diego,

Something happened today beneath the cement slabs, on hardwood floor beneath a floor, breathing alongside bodies in a dark space—lying under a net held by two Buddhas; their words brought with them an impossible blue from below. I was that color of blue—beyond the sky we found on the ocean floor. The ocean floor does not belong to anyone. You'll understand this when you're ready.

Diego,

Time is real insofar as we exist within a holographic universe.

Dear Diego,

You know they call you "una mancha oscura"? A dark stain on the history of the Yucatán; this history of colonization. La leyenda negra. You're the opposite of black lavender milk. I should've never searched your name on Twitter. I feel sick. Sick with all the weight of white people posing on the lawns where you burned off my tongue. Oh fuck. I just found an article about your ghost roaming the streets, suffering. I need to go meet (with) you; I need to take your poetry workshop on fire and regret. You burned everything because you thought we were making offerings to our gods. Hundreds were crippled or killed before you burned everything. We were just living and you tortured us. You beat us. You hung up by our wrists with stone weights, painting our bare flesh with boiling pig's fat. You raped us. You murdered us. You desecrated our ancestor's ancestor's graves. You enslaved hundreds without explanation for decades. You forced death down the throats of so many. And now I have white people to tell me about it. To tell me all about everything it is I lack. It's funny, whenever I go looking for you, I also wind up searching for my father: the sperm donor that disappeared before I was ever alive—I was just a pigment then, a small hope. I google the name and put it into f*cebook, but it's always the same: zero results found, or it's a constant search through the same too young and unfamiliar faces. When I go searching for my father, I have only my own face to help locate his image. My face, that in some ways resembles your face, which resembles no one that I know.

A.

Dear Diego,

I write to you because there's nothing else to do; nothing to be done, and yet we must go on. Go on living, go on writing, despite feeling like there's nothing coming; nothing on its way or leaving, just a stagnant sound, the hum of a lake; the creak from an angle of sky. Diego, I'm broken glass and alleyway corpse trash. Today, I'm subordinate to the ways of white folk. Today, I'm a dead end bottom shelf bank deposit. Today, I'm three days late on the rent and still a hundred dollars short. Today, I can't afford a bus to see my little brother's graduation. Today, I'm fucking tired. Today, I let the phone banker really have it, because they couldn't understand that I didn't have the money; they couldn't understand that I wouldn't have the money. Today, I let myself cry on the floor of my lungs, I cuddled right up to the bronchioles and let it out. Today, I daydreamt about punching the fridge at work until it or my hand broke. Today, I find myself writing to you because my hand is broken and I don't know how to poem. I don't know how to write anything else anymore. I've conditioned myself to write to you instead of anyone else. There's a list of emails that need sending. There's a shorter list of letters. Phone calls need returning. Appointments need to be set. And yet, here I am writing to you. You who never writes back. Except for maybe in my dreams. Maybe it was, maybe you wanted to be closer to talk more intimately. Maybe these letters just aren't doing it for you anymore. I've started reading your account in earnest, with red pen, and I realize it's more than you Diego. It's the idea of you; it's the idea you were indoctrinated with, that you were raised with. It's this fucked up notion of supremacy that keeps rearing its ugly head: this idea of being better because of inherent whiteness. The translator of your work, like most academics of his era, is a pompous white supremacist with a warped, fetishistic curiosity and sense of superiority over the indigenous. It's so funny to me, Diego, the desire to be other that stems from white people, they fetishize indigenous culture and call it fashion. I'm starting to lose the thread here, Diego. It's getting hard to keep on keeping on from where I'm standing. So much of me would rather lay down and take notes. To go on, living.

Dear Diego,

You never write back. It's been a couple of years now, or close to that, and you've yet to send me a damn word. It's frustrating really. I thought somehow, you'd welcome the correspondence, or maybe you'd ask me to write something in Spanish, but maybe you can't understand any of what I've been writing to you. Maybe you just hear your name and a strange foreign tongue when these words are spoken or when these words are sung. I'm sure that's its own kind of hell: knowing something is being said of you but not being able to decipher what; is it sinister, or is it benevolent? I don't quite know myself yet. See, I'm not entirely sure what you're for. If you have a real purpose beyond your ruin. I wonder if there's a form of angel that assesses previous judgments made on souls in the name of god— I'd like to be that kind of angel, and I'd hate to say it Diego, but I kind of feel like I'm that angel; I don't want your name spoken any longer. You're a bad man. That's all anyone will ever know of you. Unless, of course, you write back to defend yourself. Good luck with that.

A

Dear Diego,

What does it mean to be beautiful? What does it mean to speak beautifully? I used to understand this as poetry; as prayer, and then my body stopped praying, or rather my body began rejecting this tongue. The tongue I write to you in; the tongue my mother calls our "native language." But Spanish did not blossom on the Peninsula; Spanish was transmitted with violence; my blood recalls a trauma and anxiety spreads to my pupils when speaking the tongue. It sounds beautiful to some, and yet to me it sounds like a question. It sounds like a form of skin. It still sounds foreign just as all language sounds foreign, except for the language of empathy, which we all hold some form of access to. I open my mouth and it rains in California for three days straight; the air becomes a wavering cloud, the sound washes out the color until all is spectral and aglow. I touch the soil of my memory, which is sand and could once become water, but now I'm all mud. I keep finding earth in my mouth; my teeth, these accidental crystals or rotting fossils. I keep finding this want for blossom. This want for bloom. This want for something more than beautiful but healing. I want to song. To make us soft again. To bring the violence of living to a stillness; a song to cradle the traumas of our ancestries, to sleep in hopes of dreaming a means of raising the sun from its absence. I am mess of slow flowers. I want the ghosts to show themselves so that we might hold them; become a nest in which they might rest. I'm so sick of all this pain. My body is a constant struggle. My body is a stolen artifact. My body is a gulf of dreaming. My body is the result of "globalism," my body fated to suffer diaspora displacement dissociative depression disorders. My tongue is a refuge. My tongue is a foreign vessel. My tongue is a weapon. My tongue is an organ. My tongue is my song.

I forgot I was supposed to stop writing to you, but it's raining today and the grey sky reminded me of time and how we're all bound to one another across this weaving of reality and light. When you set the Maya language on fire I can't help but think you had these evil aims of erasure on your mind. It was July 12, 1562, when you decided Maní Yucatán was a proper pyre place for your auto-de-fé it was then you stopped my ability to speak beautifully and, while I hear the song in the night of my heart, I don't know the words. My body is quiet. Stripped of its mother tongue, my body is compliant. My body searches for its organs in the rubble of its oppressor. My body sifts through the language patching shards together until there is an echo of the song. The mother song. The first song still sleeping in our blood. The blood of those who remain. The blood of those who remember. Remember that there was once a song that sounded nothing like these trees. Remember there was a song that sounded something like "home." That is beautiful. That is still resting in our throats. I cut my hands in the body of my oppressor. I cut my tongue in search of dust; that dead skin that recalls a life before this language. When I bleed I can see a portal or mirror forming in the wound; I peer deeply into it until there is a vision. After the fire is a hole in the earth that reaches to 1562; it's full of ink, and I've been digging. And I'm still digging. I'm still digging I'm still digging I'm still digging I'm still digging and I'm still digging, I still

Love,
-Angel.

Dear Diego,

I can't keep working this job I'm working. It's eating my language; it's killing my soul. It's hard to know what exactly I'm trying to say, or why I'm telling you about it. I think I'm asking you for help. How do I do it? How do I escape the capitalist life—how do I reclaim this language? The language of a slow sunrise. The language of salt and blood. The language of 10,000 stones. The language of sleeping stars. The language that gives me my name. I hate the person I am when I'm working; everything is a performance to evade the suffering. I hate the suffering, everyone's suffering. It's exhausting. It hurts. It hurts so much I can't sleep at night; I can't dream late enough, always waking up with the sunrise. Just keep gathering the language together like dominoes; become a mechanism for enchantment; live the magic. That's the dream right? It's hard to know why I write to you anymore Diego. It's so strange when I write your name on a shape of whiteness, cup, document; form, or process square, it's rare. I always want to mention to that Diego that *My Diego* stole my tongue and murdered my ancestors. It's hard to know how much you should share in an email, or with a stranger. I want to tell people about you Diego, but I don't want your name in my mouth; you don't pay the bills. I don't want anyone to know about you; I want you in/as ruin. I want you as absurd curiosity because, maybe it was aliens, right? That's what they said about my people and our structures: it was aliensss mannn, it couldn't have been Black and Brown people. And, maybe you were an alien. Right? People couldn't have built those structures without white people? Well, nothing human could ever be so cruel. No one could have (tried to) exterminate a language from a people. It must have been those space specimens. The cover-ups and unidentified vessels of the white imaginary: cosmic colonizers. There's too much to explain and, really, I suck at writing letters. Oftentimes I feel like I'm rambling through caffeine tremors, soaking in a thick delirium—the awkward whimsy of the present moment. It's language. But who cares. This pile of letters. This alien heart. This figure, this fugue, this dancing.

Cheers,
X

Dear Diego,

I'm always dodging debt collectors, calling 6 times a day, waking me up and ruining my sleep cycle / I hallucinate a brief glimpse of my grandfather in the far off man that stares into himself, and thereby the sky. I vortex a heap of marijuana and try to go about my day without crying but just look at the white world around you.

This Brown body in repose is never quite in repose, always in question of who will see it, and will they be a threat—do I die today, like this?—this body full of colonization-dystrophy with its instinct to feed upon the flesh of my oppressor? How are you supposed to politely reject your suffering? Genocide is not a matter of opinion.

I feel guilty whenever I think or talk about race—I'm never well read enough to understand my own skin apparently—I've never had enough language to explain my oppression—to stain my pain into a relatable atom so that we might molecule.

So I stay quiet.

I document microaggressions. I survive microaggressions.

They pile up to form the mountain I live on, where it's quiet free from light pollution—it's where I see my breathing clearly, stolen from its ancestry, my tongue loves the shapes of its oppressor, the way it curves the globe around me into broken fragments of other sounds until there is a bridge of body language to point to what we lack. I'm always pointing towards uncertainty; I'm always pointing towards my ancestry: el cielo.

Dear Diego,

I don't think I can do it. In fact, I can't. I can't be Notre Dame, or Nice, or Paris, or anything else until I am the doing something about the suffering of my own people. I realize that this trouble stems from fetishizing globalism, or going after that whole "we are the world; just one big human family," #alllivesmatter approach. The problem is we are not. Not all lives are in danger, which is not to say that all lives don't matter, I'm just saying: white people need to sit the fuck down. Do you know what it's like to be immediately discounted based on where you come from and what you look like Diego? Difference means death. Here, I think aloud into the void of social media, something about white people continuing a distortion of Yucatec Maya history and culture, a distortion which you started btw. I post my dissent in all caps and, of course, I get nothing but white men commenting by means of correcting me, or offering me context, or sarcastically voicing their favor for white supremacy without even knowing me. At the same time, I get messages of solidarity and support from other white people. It gets so confusing. Oppression lies in socioeconomic separation as much as it lies within racial discrimination. Privilege is the true oppressor. It just so happens that those who incepted the idea of racial superiority via notions of privilege, plots of incepted religion, etc. were, and remain, colonizers. The concept of white people's affinity for cultural and historical distortion and appropriation can be likened to a locust swarm. A zombie horde of "super-predators" we'll call "the white man". The white man fancies himself a predator. The white man decided himself superior and that was that. The white man is a concept, or can be reduced to such. The white man is a vicious and frightened parasite of manipulation and oxidation. The white

28

man is a concept to be disproven. The white man is a lonesome and tragic actor warping the fabric of history. The white man is police boots and bullets and bullets and bullets and words. The white man is none of my business. The white man is the reason I'm afraid for my brothers and sisters; the white man is the reason I'm afraid for my family, and the family beyond my blood, I mean the family that looks and suffers like me. The white man is unsettled and worried about me writing all these letters of truth and tiredness. "The white man" is as flattening and inaccurate as "Hispanic." I worry for everyone who is not white. This worry confines me to my bed for hours and days at a time, shades drawn, even here up on the mountain where I live. I know I'm one of only a handful of POC that live amongst the redwoods. Confederate flags are more common than you'd expect in California; the glares and long suspicious stares are about the same as any city or space that's over run by white people. See Diego, I grew up acutely aware of my difference, I grew up knowing that I was different because of more than just my tongue. My skin said: speak to me in Spanish, or expect an accent. My skin said: hoodlum; hoodrat; down; street savvy; every block belongs to somebody; another problem for a city to throw police at. Do you know what that's like, to flow through worlds on the regular? Navigating the language that best suits the situation without having a real foundation or strategy outside of day-to-day survival.

Dear Diego,

Summer is coming and I think I'm starting to understand my family for the first time. Or, I guess I'm coming to understand where I came from more, and my responsibility to that space; how to communicate with the blood that spreads out from there. The blood that doesn't leave. How to remind them of what they really are. What we really are. I guess part of it has to do with a blurred history, smudged by fire and faith—erasure is a tricky thing Diego. You're not entirely to blame. There have been countless others since you; they're all white; it goes so far beyond the Spanish. We've become living artifacts that are dismissed and remised for tourist trap attractions and overseas laundering. We're the tropical backdrop of the colonial imaginary; a place for white people to get married. Our shores are full of spring break rapists and some, I assume, are good people. But who am I to say? I didn't grow up white, with control of history, in a deep denial about ancestral atrocities. Why do I write to you? The letters fill suitcases and drawers and piano benches. The letters distract from the days of constant struggle. The wretched torture of going on. You know something about torture. And really, while you may have strung up my ancestors from their wrists with their arms tied behind their back and burnt their flesh with boiling pig's fat, I'd wish a shift in the service industry on you. Back to back opening shifts. I wish call centers and construction jobs and all the white people on you. I wish overdraft fees and late rent worries upon you. I wish the weight of the world's whiteness on you. I'd rather you experience that than die. Because you die a little everyday with that, and still you have to press on—you have to put on that brave face that says you won't wear me down, and I doubt you have that face, Diego. I wish every late paycheck and lack

30

of food stamps on you. I wish GRE tests on you. I wish the critique of the fucking institution on you. I wish the alabaster architecture of academia on you. I wish a withering upon your wretchedness. I once wrote a postcard to someone who never got it; I hope you got it; I hope you were hungry for a language that wasn't ever yours; I hope you chewed right through your tongue trying to understand: how I wish you were here.

Kisses,
AD

Dear Diego,

The mail keeps piling up and none of it is from you. It's bills mostly; it's mostly bills I can't pay. There's nothing beautiful or strange about it. It's just a sad paper cut I keep reopening with blades of grass and wind. I dodge calls from them the way I do family members, sorry I didn't but also not that sorry. I don't like to talk on the phone unless I have to. I'd rather see you. But I do enjoy writing letters, although the number of people I've ever written letters to is really closer to a handful, and you're one of the people. But you're not my people. You're not blood. You're not fam. But I still write to you. But with you there's the dramatic irony that you're already dead, and you were never okay, and let's not forget that I basically hate you. Or, well, my feelings for you have been a tumultuous drama; now I'm indifferent. My feelings for you are subject to change. My feelings for you are spoonfuls of ash and gravel—I don't drink whiskey anymore, otherwise there'd be bottles. You're the sour turn of too many drinks morning after—head wobbling on the way to work until plateau of sunrise washes the horizon clean with color; the moon retreats into a subtle hallucination. Fingernail or full circle. You know I think you're a coward? I don't even mean that insultingly, you know: I get it. I'm a coward too sometimes. I don't write or call or text when I should and that anxiety eats me alive for days and days and weeks and weeks and months and years. It builds ulcers in my stomach or stones in the soil of the orchard. I live on an orchard now. The strange magic of writing brought me here, and here I am, still waiting to talk to you: body of my oppressor. Languid talisman of the fire—you awful stench. That smell of: I don't have enough words for you. That smell of fire that never the brain after a wildfire; the smell of soot and blood covering embers, until the sun returns to reveal a lack of color: a hole where a language should have been. An absence where, once, there was a song, or flower. That flower could have been a tree; that song could have been the sky. But I guess we'll never know, will we Diego?

Dear Diego,

When I was growing up, I was taught that the sky belonged to wealth. Travel for us was only ever for funerals, and even then, if you couldn't afford to drive there you wouldn't go there. Travel belonged to white people on TV, because they had the money; they had the entirety of the Western world; its legacy, on their side. Every history book that had ever been standardized and placed in front of me read: white savior. Read: you love globalism. The movies said the same thing. You'll learn to be white, Brown body, if only you try hard enough. You have to really "try." Then you can fly. Then you can travel to other lands and say, fuck this and fuck that. Then you can colonize. Just never forget, you are not and will never be white. And while globalism may have opened doors and windows across the world, the architecture, the house, still belongs to the white man amalgam who fancies himself a "master." The house is not yours. The handrails and banisters and stairs are not for you. For you is the labor of learning what was stolen from you. Cleaning the house and learning its history. Your work is to sit with this until you die. Your work is to work and never question why you work. Your work is to die nameless, providing the basis for statistics, and hashtags. This way, empire can say: the Brown body was killed of its own accord. The brown body died in poverty because the brown body did not try hard enough. And when I did try. When I did. It didn't fucking matter. I am the scene of an absent sun. I am airplane growl. I am not who they want me to be. I am rage. I am many and I am ready. Ready to enter the earth as a meteor. To rewrite the living ledger of history. To dismantle and destroy white supremacy.

To rip the face off my enemy until they understand.

Xo,
Tu Sangre

Dear Diego,

I contemplate the weight of race while an ambulance blares.
I get lost in the oil-stained asphalt.

I look out to passing buses recognizing bodies in transit but,
I don't play by that racquet—don't live like that anymore.

When surrounded by white bodies, it's always easy to pick
up on the subtleties; the stare of a smile, the violent act in the
"accident."

I don't lift my eyes to the coming transport—the pigeons are
the same; my spine still bristles at the sight of a policeman in
too close a proximity for comfort—I've done nothing wrong
but live marked as a Brown vessel, expendable, and threaten-
ing the all amerikkkan's dreams.

I'm always sitting next to white people, it seems I'm something
of an oddity or attraction—*how's it God made you again, a lit-
tle too close to the sun? a little too savage to know Jesus died for
your sins? a little too animal to speak European tongue? Where
is it that you come from? But before that?* When prompted for
response, I mostly just growl to myself until they look the oth-
er way.

I have learned to become what is required of me.

Dear Diego,

I eat my breakfast as the language family of the words tear themselves apart; I write a little letter to you in my head with the bits of green and gold flecks left over from the rubble of the conversation. I lend you an armful of water, mineral rich, and yes, I left the mud for you. I need you to taste flesh of my suffering. It is like the earth in that its end is inevitable. I need you to taste my anxieties, they cripple me and I say nothing; it's this granular little raspiness in my voice when I try to speak; it's that river water that ruins me. I offer you water to show I'm not a threat. I offer you water to show I know what we need in the world to be alive. Empathy like water. Nightmares calm down when you have a sip. Sit up in a dark cube and wonder how you wound up here, head against the moonlight. You both embody a darkness that hums quietly like a calming song. I refuse the song of colonialism though my chains of lease and lonesomeness are Euro-made, I fall victim to the beast of capitalism; I fall victim to Americanism; I fall victim to the crushing defeat of my ancestors. I fall victim to all my failures; I fall victim to my words; my language crumples itself into an asthma attack and I cease all bronchial functions in a panic: this is how I get closer to you.

Diego,

There is no book without the land; without the land there is no language.

        There is no site for the event to have taken place.

Dead Diego,

You are the boat that gets left behind and set ablaze. Enemy boat on fire along the shore.

My tongue is my enemy. My tongue is my body. My tongue is my refuge, my tongue is my home. My tongue is a safe space until I get faded; then I'm dangerous, then I'm lung capacity thick, gone like fire burning down Gaudí's cathedrals until they're pyramidal rubble.

You return to places to recreate them. You revenge a sense of validity from memory; disperse the ghost mentality of never again and withdraw yr jaws from oppressor's hands. There's nothing but bone now. Clear breakpoints to dismantle the architecture. Here we crease at the sentence; fold the white away and what we are left with is night. The sun will rise without us.

Dear Diego,

Today's the day and I can't print you. How did you work out
your defense for atrocities against the indigenous on your way
home? How much paper did you have? What ink? Did you
resort to blood, urine, or semen? There's a million things you
have me wondering about these days. It seems our similarities
just keep piling up. Both our lungs asthmatic; both our hands
writing. What does it mean to share commonalities with the
root of your oppression? Do you share a likeness with your
oppressor? Is this a type of Stockholm syndrome I've devel-
oped for you, or are we kin Diego? What's the difference when
I rehearse the sound of you in my head, just as you must have,
writing your *Relación* from memory.

Santo pendejo madre de Mestizx,
ruegas por nosotros, los pecadores con pulmones,
los desgraciados de tus pecados
ahora y en la hora de nuestra muerte, Amén.

Dear Diego,

I wrote to the encyclopedia Britannica until they changed their language. I wrote:

This article is proliferating a false history of the Yucatec Maya people and the suffering they endured under the reign of this awful friar, who actually did nothing to help the Maya people and even went so far as to forge letters and signatures of the indigenous during his trial with the Spanish crown. Your article is doing a disservice to the descendants of those who suffered, who were murdered and enslaved by this awful man. This needs to be corrected immediately. The distortion of history is a form of oppression that you are compliant with by publishing this article as is.

Angel Dominguez,
Thank you for contributing to Encyclopedia Britannica. Upon review, our editors have revised the entry "Diego de Landa" to incorporate the changes that you suggested, with some modifications and additions.
We greatly appreciate your help in improving the quality of the information on our site. In acknowledgment, we've credited you as a contributor to the article:
https://www.britannica.com/biography/Diego-de-Landa/ article-contributors.
Best,
Readers' Editor, Encyclopaedia Britannica

Slowly, you're becoming more legible…
a.

Dear Diego,

I've stopped writing to you altogether now; now there's very little (time) to write to you. I lost that notebook where I'd write to you by hand near the end of it, and even then I think that we weren't going anywhere anymore. I guess this is a break up letter. I'm letting you go. It's nothing personal aside from I fucking hate you and want nothing to do with you. I don't care that you finally wrote back. I don't care that we were communicating with energy and shape more than language. I don't care that I've come to understand that you manifest as a pestering insect or garbage stuck in the sand. Maybe we had to clasp hands for a brief moment, if only in passing. I wanted so much for us Diego. I wanted atonement to rain softly through us both until we were better weather. I wanted to know that there was some purpose to this continuous suffering. I built a nest of words and spoke nothing but puro fuego. It's in this way I sabotaged myself, with shade and fire. It was this way for as long as I wrote you letters and for years before that. We don't talk about those days now. Goddamnit Diego. I just wanted a quick kiss in the autumn wind with aspens all around us, beside an ocean. I wanted blue talk to blush when your scruff rubbed my skin warm and pink link oppressor. Wanted you to sleep beside me like too many tumblers left us stumbling through oil-painted midnight. We were a durational study of love across several centuries and I must say we had a decent "will they or won't they" going there for a bit, but you wouldn't and won't and that's it. There's a lot that goes into writing to you. I deposit so much of myself into your vacuum. I hurt until the plateau hits. I hang out until I'm all out; I was all in for you, Diego. I was always all in with every body I ever encountered.

Somewhere along the way of writing to you I learned adding bodies to my own didn't ever make me warmer. I was always absent of something; always seeking out a warmth to substitute my own. I wanted to be a little dimmer than I was. Wanted to sound out a different language than the one I was given. I'm still practicing the words that don't make sense; it's these missteps I return to when returning that way. The water's frozen but I can make out your body now. You're buried under my own skeleton. You're implied when I am identified. "Hispanic," don't panic, this is only paper work; it shouldn't matter that you're categorized into the body of your oppressor, you're just another remora for the predators of the globe. Fuck your freshwater. Fuck all that minor key language. Fuck that down low low down on the reality of the universe. You'll think linearly from now on. Nothing is a spiral. You're another other from the birth canal of conquest. You're just a moon to stick a flag in. You're a plant that we mowed down in favor of good ole Kentuckybluegrass. So what if this is California. So what if this is Aztlán; Alta Califas; Mayapán; Yucatán, amerikkka whatever. What are you going to do about it? Diego, what are we going to do about it? I want all the artifacts back. Museums are a fucking lie. I want my language back. I want to reconcile the many afterlives of colonization that keep raging inside of me; I want to know a love like the burn of belts and chanclas, the RNA memories handed down from flogging and being flogged by our ancestors. I want to know the love of forgiveness. Like how do you put down a dog that attacked you? How do I put you to bed while pulling you back into my blood?

Like a reverse exorcism, I'm calling you into my body. Stay with me.

43

I'm inviting you home. I don't want more fighting. I just want to atone atone atone atone atone atone alone. No more of this public squabble. No more of these late nights acting like I don't love you. Like you don't love me.

This can be real.

Diego,

My darling, did you really think your empire could ever end me?

Dear Diego,

What are we? Symbiotic or codependent? How do you cope with someone who's been gaslighting you for centuries? You're not capable of imposter syndrome Diego. Moreover, you've been a stone skipping for far too long. It's time to sink. I let you sink into me until the blood of my family is soaked with your name. Until my heritage is so distressed I place an X upon a self-made word. I let you sink into me while refusing to mark "Hispanic" on any form; everything gets marked "other." Am I still other to you Diego, despite all these letters? Despite all our history? I'm trying to reprogram the way I listen to my mother tongue. I'm trying to learn the language of absence and recuperation. I'm having to double back threefold to get to the start. It's all language and tongue in constant decay, piling up an accumulation of mud in the December rain. The tongue folds down again, back into the earth; it soaks into the sky above it. Above our sky is a history stored in earth crystal: we call them clouds now, we call them heaven sent some times; sometimes, it's the apocalypse at our door Diego. When I go searching for what remains of you, I seek out what I fail to see in me, for I too am complicit, taking French instead of Spanish; never keeping up with either because poverty taught me English is your only way out or up in this globalist-society. Reject your family tongue because that's what keeps them under white architecture, holding it up with their exhausted blood for generations. I see how I fail to incorporate my obsession with you into anything useful. The cloud keeps piling up with letters to you. They rain down into a small black rectangle that stays in my pocket. I keep your coffin close to me. I use new world magic the way you used inquisitional tactics; I'll torture you with what you don't know, nail your tongue down to the earth

with a keystroke; I'll make a clay oven from Pepsi factory bottle;
I'll regurgitate your act-of-faith-fire, and show you a language
of stars.

Love,
A

Dear Diego,

It's been determined that we might be needing each other for
the time being; I keep returning and rereading your remem-
brance, and it's hilarious. It's hilarious how it reminds me that
nothing in history matters. Time comes down to Bergson, bro-
ken down into Platonian notions/motions; it's really a matter
of our remarkable points. Fuck all the swirly stuff that comes
before and after. It's a matter of magnets. We were drawn to
one another without knowing. Like soul mates. Can you be
soul mates with a dead person you've never met? With some-
one who destroyed your culture? Who destroyed your moth-
er's mother's mother's ancestor's tongue? Can we be in love,
Diego, or is this a strictly one-way relationship? You know I
love to give you words like flowers, even when they're full of
thorns or foxtail ferns. My ikebana is a messy one. I provide
dirt where there should be water. Me, I'm that spot of ash or
soot, the thing mistook for shadow, when really I'm remnant.
See Diego, I'm what's left over from your auto-de-fé Call me
Xix. Remnant. Residue. Xix. Pronounced "sheesh." Your act-
of-faith gave birth to the world that birthed me; you're a pillar
of charcoal, and I'm just a refracted memory existing both now
and in future memory. I'm your molecule as much as you are
mine. I am all that remained when you swept our bodies away
into the wind. I'm that last bit of you left to say the thing.

A. Out.

Dear Diego,

What are the words? What are the words that poison me? Words like poor; words like war; words that no one can agree on; Latine/Latinx/Brown/How—how to unmake all this anti-Blackness with(in) words? I'm lost in a bevy of constant linguistic detritus, reaching for what's not there. Reaching for what was once more than ruin. You know I dated ruin once; was in bad for the worst. I let myself dive down to those Scorpio depths I'd been warned about: down to the bottom stone cold of a meticulous auto-immolation by way of language, and time. Does it matter? Diego, the sun is often fire, but sometimes soft. Clouds perpetuate a cold light that resembles the left cheek of the moon. I suppose there's a lot that resembles distance. Language for instance. We fold temporal tracts. We're coexistent in this moment, Diego; where you are is where I am, and we're both suffering. Ultimately, to imagine a binary is to destroy the true nature of reality. A growing wave function. Maybe I want to grow with you, to learn how to seize the means of production. How to grow gardens with micro-grid permaculture resilience? Maybe then we could grow to understand one another. Ultimately, you're an asteroid that fossilized my sense of self into a distance I live with every day. The dreaming is a part of it, but mainly it's words. The first words aren't always best. Sometimes, they take centuries to gestate and reincarnate into an antibody attack upon colonial systems born of the invasion, and desecration of ancestral kin. It's in this way I recognize our need to disarm one another, and maybe have a glass of wine or something. It's hard to get the words out when first reflex is murder or something of the sort. It seems I've always got questions for you Diego. Like you know. Like in death the Big questions get answered, so I expect you to return some knowledge in exchange for what you stole. So what are the words, Diego? What are the words that have poisoned me, and is there an antidote, or am I simply retching? Kiss me before I vomit. I can hold my own hair back, but Diego, I can't find the words anywhere anymore. I'm constantly plugged into an architecture of oppression, acting as a beautiful cog in the machine. My office door reads: beautiful cog in the machine, and no one asks any questions. I haven't the language to work it all out. Couldn't write a syllabus to save my life, or yours for that matter. What are the words what are the words what are the words?

Dear Diego,

I don't know why I want to destroy myself so often. There's an undeniable predilection towards oblivion. Perhaps it's the hot blood of youth, cooling. It's an unnavigable infatuation; I orbit the edge of my wounds so they never really heal. My wounds won't ever heal because I constantly pick at them; even if only their peripheries. I don't know if the wounds are intact but they sometimes throb. Like a tooth that should have been taken out, I tongue the tender parts of myself until something breaks. How else do I say this Diego? I, too, can be monstrous. What is this dark electricity of the body that propels us towards each other? I don't understand my own fatalistic drive towards an inevitably terminal point. I crashed the airplane in my first book. I don't think you know this, but the last time I was writing a book, I tried to return myself to the earth several times. Or at least, I tried to get as close to letting go as possible. I swam against creeks and rivers until I felt like a stone. Diego, like you, I've hurt a lot of people. It's not just that I have been hurt by people. It's that I myself have taken a role in the suffering of others. Writing to you is a form of confession. I used to burn all my manuscripts. Diego, are you the reason I used to set everything I wrote on fire? Are you my process? Did you get my letters when I burnt them? Do you miss me like I miss you?

Dear Diego,

The moments pop out like crystals. Fully formed in the dirt before their emergence; only revealed by mud. Rain reprograms the unknowns with ancestral memory. The scope of their mystery widens to hold the crystal-smeared sky, tiny prisms of temperature divide the color scheme into recollections of other skies and other times. The language grows right out of the earth. We breathe it in while sleeping. I shape it all day long, chewing up the words and swirling them around my circadian coasting. I deposit short poems into my ligaments so that poetry continues to keep me together when I am weak. The ligaments strain from overuse and must be soothed regularly lest they snap. I am a temporary distance, glittering.

Dear Diego,

Why do I even write to you? Dear Diego. The year is twenty-nothing and my own people hate me, see they've equated Westernized intelligence with whiteness and told me to go to school; two white pieces of paper later and I am no better than you: our colonizer. And aren't you in my blood? Doesn't Dominguez come from Spain? But where did I come from? Los Angeles, right? Born in a time between riots. Before the movie company tore down our immigrant home in favor of a flat patch of night; in Hollywood—parking lots are profitable—but no one parks upon the outline of our bloodline. Our house was destroyed for nothing. Diego, I want to be sipping pints of your blood while you talk to me about Jesus—I want you to save my soul while I hold you against the bottom of a dzonot. Let's become flowers in the ashes of Maní, Yucatán together. Come sleep with me, in the garden of my bedroom; I want you to wilt like funeral rose, into something I keep forever. Proof that, at one time, someone I love died—I was there—in mourning. Proof that I haven't forgotten that pain. The rose becomes a black bit of lace at the foot of a funeral program. Maybe we can learn to call this intimacy; won't you join me in my bedroom?

Dear Diego,

All our undulations become lines; I used to think in wave-length, but solidified in favor of semantic articulations, in appreciation of the warm and buoyant void. I misplaced you somewhere inside of my system; I can taste your sweat when I cough into the skin of my elbow; I can taste your tongue lingering on my every word in Spanish. I hoist you up into my spinal column until you've infected all of me: call me patient zero for colonial dystrophy: accessing the genome of oppression across forty screens to see the entirety of the human blueprint, parsed out into columns and letters and colors. We look like angles trapped in a white grid when we look at ourselves in this way: there is so much space between you and I, Diego, despite the distance you and I are alleles of one another.

I X out your Y.

Always softening the inherited violence of machismo with a queer heart.

Always yrs,
A

Dear Diego,

I often think about when I used to teach, how special that time in the classroom really was; the ways in which the students themselves taught me and teach me. Everyone with a seat at the table. A horizontal discussion of whether or not we even need the table. It was of the upmost importance to me to imbue my students with this notion: knowledge is created together, it's not something you download or deposit into your consciousness. It's a conversation. It was important to me to remind my students of their humanity. Always hoping that in some small way I might tip them off to the falseness of the capitalist pyramid scheme. The importance of maintaining our creativity. Reminding them that no one deserves to die in a field or factory. It doesn't have to be this way. We attempt to identify the ways in which Whiteness perpetuates non-white human suffering; this means having to untangle the system of systems from the genetic phenotype. It's important to me that my students understand how white supremacy is not simply a kind of phenotypical disposition held by white people. Much like empathy, this behavior and its toxic beliefs, are learned. They are taught and reinforced. It's not something anyone is born with. I wonder if you knew of whiteness when you were still breathing, Diego. I wonder if you understand what I mean by whiteness, when you read it now?

Dear Diego,

I've thought long and hard about what you are. Clawed my way
through your body until most of you was moss and rot and ash.
I read a translation left behind by some white guy and really
just glanced through what of yours was found. Out of order,
sections missing. It looked a lot like all of history. It was hard to
care or take it seriously and while the translator was so proud
of himself for obtaining these tax documents of the Yucatán, I
was far more taken with the letters written by the indigenous.
Two letters made me cry on the beach, muttering in blue speak.
They said things I didn't know and it hurt me. It hurt in the
way you feel your grandmother's marrow weaken with time.
It hurt in the way every regret accumulates in your body on
the worst days. It hurt in the way that you can remember, but
not relive. Being unable to aid your blood in its struggle. The
cancer of poverty destroying your family, and what are you but
a pile of woozy words. You're just burdened with knowledge
and nothing more. Diego. Why did you paint boiling fat onto
our bare flesh? Why did you dislocate our shoulders with ropes
and weights? Why did you dismantle our sleeping dead with
shovels and fire? Why did you enslave us for eight to ten plus
years without explanation? And what of the rapes and beat-
ings in every pueblo? What of the fire? I hope weight of our
blood crushed your wicked heart. A river grows over the site
of what's left. A language returned with water instead of fire
or blood; we flood the furnace away, we reverse the bonfires
and recoup our scar tissue. Down to the raw materials, we are
eternal. Diego, I am not afraid of you any longer. I know your
scent; its sound, when you start to creep in from infinity. We're
magnetic, you and I. Bound together by blood and time. We
are a time of day. A dim paradise. We're bound at the mouth,

your lips are always on mine; when I speak, your voice comes through in concentric circles. We're synonyms for one another; I can never quite make out which of us is the meaning. Always exchanging language and fire, like binary stars before oblivion. Won't you just end us with me? Just this once, please:

burn   after   reading.

Diego,

Estx es para todxs Mestizx, que son sangre de mi sangre, y que brillan como la luna...

Dear Diego,

You could say, I've been in search of a séance. The longer I'm at it the more estranged I become from my body; the more it's this refracted process through which I view the world, with you looking back at me in the mirror. I spend every day contemplating the radiation decay of colonization; I spend every day acutely aware of my "race" and my complex blood, the way its molecular composition is representative of so much more than just my own body. We're linked, you and I. It happens when we language: I give and you give and we connect in an instant, what was I supposed to give you? Diego, I'm not talking to you now. I'm talking to you, now. What am I supposed to write to you? I guess I want to spread my blood thin enough to be a compass. I want to figure it out in front of you. It's not always about mourning, or trauma, or healing even. Sometimes, we are alive, and that can be enough. There is a magic to the quotidian; a beauty in the banal. It doesn't all have to be a poem. It doesn't all have to be meaningful. Sometimes, it's just you, living. And that's enough. How is it we unfold the language into a feeling? How do we use language to summon the dead? I only want to language. But which tongue? Which tongue do you choose when you want to talk to the dead? Which tongue? Which tongue? Which tongue?

Dear Diego,

I keep walking through walls and bumping into things; it's things like capitalism, colonization, and the ever-present threat of white supremacy. Diego, soy diamante. Diego, I am a landslide. A mountain of mud and rain ready to run down redwoods across roadways and out into the ocean. Diego, I've been talking to you for a long time. It seems we never quite catch each other at the right time; our calendars have always been out of sync. It's hard to make time to forgive you. It's been all these years and I still don't know if I want to forgive you. I don't think it works like that. I think I love you; our love is a blackberry bramble. You know blackberries grow out here, earlier every year. They're an invasive species, much like myself; I love blackberries. I let their brambles take my blood when I cull the color from the vine. I can't tell which of us is violent. I can only tell that there is blood and I am bleeding, but it's okay when it happens because there is nourishment. I am nourished by that which harms me. How have you nourished me, Diego? What have you done in exchange for the blood I've given up? You, blood of my blood. Flesh of my Flesh. What have you done? I've run myself rock-bottom-ragged and back; had heart murmurs and panic attacks; did a whole lot of driving; commuting on buses, trains, plains, and foot just to pull your corpse out the grave. Out of my own flesh and blood. I don a coat of lavender mold. I make a mask out of broken nouns and signifiers. I become a field of English to survive my day. To write these letters. I'm writing letters to a dead man. I'm writing letters to the ghost of my oppressor. My ancestor-oppressor. My own flesh and blood. I'm never not writing to or with you. There's a constant knowing we're sewn together into the bottom of our soles. One of us must be shadow. I know I can't escape you. I know I have to live with you. I exist despite you. I live to spite you. More than four hundred years later and here we are still fighting to figure myself out of language. Still fighting to find my reflection in the wreckage of your malice. Fighting to find a word for what I am. All these years later I wonder if I am still Maya. Mestizx, sure, but my Grandmother called our blood and my spirit Maya; my bones: Maya. My grandmother knows more than the disembodied heads of academic authority. My grandmother remembers. The temples may be ruins but we, the ongoing blood of our ancestors; the descendants of genocidal oppression; the descendants of the survivors of the invasion. While tired and poor, while hungry; while working shitty jobs we don't want, to participate in a society that doesn't want us. We are still here. We are alive, and every day we continue to grow like roses under snow. The cold cowardly whiteness of the world hopes we'll die, or forget our color under the immense pressure of its fictitious totality. Winter always thinks it will never end. And yet, we climb like roses and ivy, singing wildly; fiercely abloom and summoning the future. Kin of the Sun.

xoxo,
Roses

Dear Diego,

The world is going to end before I ever stop writing to you. Diego, the problem is that we don't want it enough; it's that it doesn't matter enough anymore to make sense. The trouble is that we're a global antibody attacking life as a disease. The trouble is that Spain still has the only surviving documents from your little campfire. The problem is that there's no one that sees this as a problem. We're still just acting like Spain didn't commit cultural and literal genocide on indigenous peoples of the Americas. We're still acting like conquest was fun and games and colonialism was the best thing to happen since shitting indoors. Idk when that took place really, it just sounded right; that sounds kind of like your reasoning/logic when devastating a people. Assess the other as other and reflex with obliteration. Devise a mediated response of self-criticism and shame, this is your fault after all. That's what colonialism taught us. Not only were we damned from the start, we chose this life. Thankfully, the Spanish came to tell us how bad we should have been feeling for their eternity, unbeknownst to them, we'd already survived several spiraled eternities and theirs was simply one of many. But their tongues couldn't bend that way. Instead, they'd thistle out a lisped letter that sounded less like our x and dz and other such sounds I won't tease you with now. You were a pound of agate when I found you, Diego. You were just ancient fire. You were fossilized in my marrow, I saw to the start of you, nothing left to hide when you're dead, and I'm not too keen on hearing you out to tell the truth. I keep wrestling with it: this tilt in my body. See, I'm not Hispanic, not Indigenous, nor Xicanx/Latinx; not part of the amerikkkan empire, but I feel something that must be similar to being alive. I lack a language to define myself because you mixed our blood and took our tongue. You developed my photograph with nothing more than accidental flame. Just a wisp of what was once two thousand years. You made me nothing but rocks. Nothing but sonic locational discovery site; vacation destination; wonder of the world. You made me nothing more but a keychain; headache; never-worn shirt; shot glass; piece of crap souvenir for others to store stories in.

Dear Diego,

I'll call you when it's over. I'll sing to you if it's done; we'll skip over all of August and the past few hundred years. We'll reconstruct the notebooks and fill station wagons with sand and slow moments that pass over the rest of what's left. Diego, I need you to sing for me, I need you to come close and dance slow; I want you to hold me because I don't think this pile of letters will ever be a book, and it hurts to know I've made you a part of me. I want to know that, maybe, at the root of everything, there was a sense of divine love, and maybe it's been long enough. No. I don't think that's a thing actually. Actually, I'll do this alone.

Dear Diego,

Keep your hands up. I never know if we're fighting or about to fuck. Sweat on sweat. Tooth to flesh. We keep on circling each other like twin sharks in a mermaid purse. Sometimes, I think I am a haunted house on the brink of collapse and you are the lonesome ghost that won't let me. I think about how, growing up, I would get so angry that I would burst into tears. My anger would wash out into an overwhelming sadness. A deep depression in the disappointment of it all. I never wanted to "win," and yet that's what this whole house of glass is predicated upon. Haves and have-nots, and nothing is more dehumanizing than money. All of it imaginary. Triggered by the onslaught of sun, there's nowhere to run when the entire planet is warming. How big a compost bin must I dig to fit the department of defense in it? How deep must I dig to bury the 3k's that hold up this nation-nightmare? How many times do I need to die to get out from under the fallacy of white supremacy? Who am I even fighting anymore? I'm afraid to use words like "us" because I honestly don't know what that means anymore. Always feels like I'm fighting, feeling the fists of my great-great-grandfather in a Yucatán ring, moving like a hurricane, folding foos like blades of grass underfoot. Feels like I am always on the floor of my consciousness, blood in my eye, trying to rally a comeback. Constantly punching at the foundations of my own family to get to the root of everything. A fist cannot dig as well as an open hand. And so I go searching for water in the soil of my heart. Trying to tour guide myself back to my base origins. Always afraid of what I'll find. Worry always on my mind. It stresses me out to think about how to best pronounce myself. Always wondering what the words might be to best see myself clearly. Sometimes, I think, eventually, I'll find your tongue,

65

golden, riddled with roaches and diamonds, and buried in one of these three billion spiral staircases that make a map of my genome. When I finally figure you out. When I finally find you. I will never, ever, let you go.

Dear Diego,

You're the only way I can poem anymore, and it's not even a poem. Diego there's so many things. The streets are full of displaced people living the post apocalypse and I am so full of rage and sorrow that it spoils into rotting pool of language. I struggle through the excess of feelings and find the approximations in the putrid before it's petrified. I don a coat of lavender mold. I don a coat of mestizx skin; I don a coat of English to get through my day. I shed the bit of you that's left in me and I pay full price for most all my sins. Often this means years of repressed shame and guilt manifesting as mistakes and messes. I make a pound of flesh out of the remnant ballad that is your name. I write until you're real and disposable. I write until I can throw you away, and if you're a failure then it's your failure and I've no part in it. Diego, I want to talk to you about white people but it's so hard. It's so hard because I'm finding it difficult in differentiating between white people and "the colonizer." I say that knowing you don't know what I'm talking about. But context is irrelevant to you; I doubt you afforded the Maya the benefit of context and, anyways, I guess context is irrelevant when it comes to genocide. There's no real way to defend that. Like: I ripped your tongue out so you could pass on the memory of loss to all those beyond you: I want you to remember that you're missing something, not the why, just the what. This is what you lack. This is what you lost. This is what you never had. This is the memory of a melody you can't put your finger on; the song has no name just as the ocean has no name; both will haunt you so long as you live. Diego, I'm a blood comet. I'm a cold riot-skin break glass lung tongue; I am so much goddamned fire. I am the fire you started five hundred years ago. I dipped my Catholicism into the water until it drowned; I was replaced with the memory of water; the first rain in Maní that washed you away back to Spain. I grit my teeth until the crack snaps tooth in half; I yank out the bone for a pint of blood I drink back down; I mountain up the residue until it develops extremes, or the capacity for such. I don't look back when I write these letters to you because I feel no need to recover the loss of language   expelled.

Dear Diego,

Something strange has been happening and I don't quite know
what to make of it—there's a wind about these days. I stopped
writing to you for a number of reasons; mainly
It's because I have no time.

I never even finished this letter, and still don't know how—it's
been a few weeks and here I am at two in the morning playing
catch up with everything I'm doing; I'm never here. I can't be;
this is what I always say—I wish I could but I can't. So I don't.
What's the point in writing to you anymore? You won't listen.
You don't understand. You don't care. You're what did this to
many, not just me. You broke it. You stole it. You still haven't
given it back. I'd love to set you on fire Diego. I don't know
why I'm still up, writing text messages and emails to you. Still
can't sleep and still I'm thinking there's nothing for me here;
maybe this is another failure. What the fuck is the point. I don't
care if you write back anymore, or visit or call. Keep it. Keep
your image; your language your limits. I'll go on remembering
what's been stripped from me; I'll clothe myself in my bloods
astronomy; locate small stars in the debt of my tongue.

Dear,

My only living grandfather is leaving to Guadalajara today; he doesn't know that he's not coming back. My grandfather, tough as nails, who fell from his roof at the age of sixty five, only to call my mother and say: "Listen, I know you're going to find out sooner or later so I figured I would call you first, I fell off my roof while re-shingling it, and I'm fine. It hurts to breathe but I'm fine." My (step)father tells me he's had dementia for the last two years, and while he's not getting worse, he's not getting better. He didn't remember who my sister was. My grandfather lost his house last week, being unable to make the payments; they took the house from him. So he's going back to Mexico. I found all this out from a stray f*cebook post that mentioned his leaving; the house leaving. The house that had been in the other side of my family for over forty years, that raised my step father and his siblings. The house where Tata (my grandfather) made a home, grew a garden; kept a semblance of dreaming alive. I wasn't able to make it down to see him in time. (Later, when he would finally go on beyond the veil, this too would be the case: too late to make the map fold into goodbye.) Mainly because no one told me he was leaving, and in part because I'm unemployed and shit broke without more than ten dollars to my name, if that. He's on his way to his gate right now, if he's not already there. Headed to Guadalajara, after the hurricane. It's 9:51 in the morning right now. He leaves at 10:00. I called my stepfather this morning in hopes of talking with my grandfather before he left. We hadn't spoken since he disowned me in a voicemail years ago, but I would speak with any evil to get to my grandfather. This brought on some unexpected anxieties: what if he doesn't remember me, or recognize my voice? What if my Spanish has deteriorated to a point of gringo turista, who can hardly ask where something is? The family was sitting down for breakfast. My stepdad passed him the phone, and he remembered me; I remembered my Spanish. We talked. He asked if I would be coming to breakfast, if I was on my way and my heart broke. No, I said, I'm too far from you right now, but soon, we'll see each other. I told him I'd grown up to become a poet, that I had a book that was being published; I promised to send him one. He asked me if I was getting married yet, he laughed and asked if it was that I was scared to go through with it and have kids. He said he was going on this trip, for a short while, and then he would be back, to stay. I told him I'd meet him the day he got back; we could go anywhere, do whatever he wanted. I even said I'd take him to church, we'd spend a Sunday going to Iglesia; I would pray right alongside him. And then he trailed off and saying goodbye became diffi- cult. We said we loved each other and that we would see each other soon; I said que Dios lo bendiga and thought of the day I would take him to church, my grandfather the Guadalupano, who so loved the Virgin that spoke Nahuatl. Once my stepdad got the phone back, he let me know: Tata doesn't know he's not coming back, he's going there to stay. His dementia won't let him realize that. He's been forgetting things, where or when he is; he forgets who he's talking to, but he always remembers you. He always asks about you, and sometimes he'll say he just spoke with you. He never forgets you. And I cry, I cry. I cry I cry. I remember saying goodbye to my Xix, my grandfather now gone beyond a decade; I promised the Yucatán, and now with Tata, my only living grandfather, I promised church. I got so sad I thought I might just go to church today and kneel at the pews until my legs fell asleep or until I felt something. But I can hardly get myself to do anything. It's just fucked up, this other deportation of consciousness. The last house of family is gone, probably to be sold to some young yuppie taking over the Culver City slums with scooter rentals and citizen patrols. I hope the avocado tree bears no fruit for them; I hope the roses wilt and die; I hope the house collapses on their white lives. It's 10 a.m. and he's on an airplane. I'm never going to see him again. I can't explain what it meant to just hear his voice. The strongest man I know, heart tougher than shark skin. He was my Tata, my grandfather who asked me to feel his hands, how'd they'd cracked and calloused and roughened up to sandpaper; he told me to go to school and become something; to never be in the fields, to never be on a construction site; he wanted me to survive. That's why I continue. I have to.

Diego, I didn't know who else to write to.

Diego,

I am only ever trying to remember.

Dear Diego,

It turns out you were born in Cifuentes, Guadalajara, Spain, a small town of two rivers and not much more; you were 130 km outside of Madrid, where you'd return to stand trial for having traveled 8,151 km to torture and "save" my ancestors, those who would die so that I could suffer the constant psychological displacement and geographical dissociation.

I wrote that right after a water ritual: *Ask the water a question.* So I asked about you; I swam until I thought I might drown. I moved back and forth until I was too exhausted to continue; I heard your voice in my head; I heard you in the water, talking to me. You never wrote back but explained why; you mentioned that you were unable to write back or read what was written. You said, *Dear angel, did you know that I too liked to swim? I grew up swimming in the local rivers, the streams and creeks.* You described your current situation, your inability to read my letters; you hoped that they were letters of encouragement or well wishing. *There is no language here; here we have no tongues. We can't understand anything and, yes, we too are still seeking an answer. I don't believe in god anymore if that's what you're wondering.* These are some of the things you said in that letter I transcribed after getting out of the water, dripping into my notebook, which has since been lost. I learned something about you from the water, from the memory of the earth that has moved from soil to soil, pushed up at the cusp of the pacific. You told me you couldn't read my letters, and that you had been meaning to write to me. A bird tore out your eyes every morning, or maybe I just wanted this for you; I do remember that the only way you were able to communicate with me was with blood. At the end of your letter you apologized for not being able to write more but you'd run out of blood. I believed you. I lost your letter Diego. I lost a lot of letters in a moment of carelessness. I attempted another kind of ritual: walk through the desert of your youth; walk through the wasteland of where you come from in 100 degree weather. Walk until you have answers. Walk until you have language. I walked seven miles and found nothing. I walked until I couldn't feel my body. I walked until I thought I might write to you, then I forgot to. I forgot the notebook at the foot of the portal. I ran for fish tacos instead. I lost every sketch. Every poem. I lost what I thought was my return to writing on the page. Now it comes back to me in bits and pieces, in constellations and waves. I read the pattern until there's a trace of the next thing. Always following the writing, knowing that, ultimately, the writing knows better than we do. We're ultimately the ones passing through.

Dear Diego,

The power is out again. The ocean is on fire again. Or, the stove light won't turn on and there is no reception or WiFi available. There is no electricity. There is a fire some 10 miles away, maybe less. The grassy lip of the Pacific caught fire from a sudden storm of 11,000 lightning strikes taking 86,509 acres over too many weeks. I was supposed to send some important emails today. One about you. And this one to you.

I'm tired of speaking from beyond the grave. Tired of the language boomerang that trago de fuego que nunca para. Tired of the desert. Tired of the weight these organs carry. Tired of translating and interpreting. Tired of language. Tired of suffering. Tired of the many-headed hydra that is colonization. Tired of its 10,000 heads and their families of ignorance and their 10,000 demon heads. Tired of these screaming tomatoes. Tired of the corpses pouring out of my pocket. Tired of bathing in the blood of my enemies, for their blood floats atop an ocean of our kin. Tired of these fractions & divisions. Tired of trying to tell the truth about a bunch of devils. Tired of talking my way thru this white world. Tired of all the poison sloshing around everyone's heads. Tired of the bag. Tired of the back and forth. Tired of the eternal bruise. This open wound that's become a canyon to gaze into. Tired of the gaze. The way these colonizers look at me, demanding that I fit their insecurities. Demanding everything of me and having the nerve to ask me why I'm so tired. I'm tired of being tired. Tired of smashing these memories of ancestry and death and displacement against my face. Tired of my face. Tired of the discourse. Tired of the talking. Tired of the fires. Tired of death. I'm tired of dying. I am tired of many things, and yet, fighting is not one of them, Diego. I don't care if I can't win. I don't care if I won't see it myself. I am what lies beyond oblivion. And I am forever.

There was a set of three days where we lived upon the surface of Mars—oxygen thin and so much smoke I lost my sense of time and place. It looks like we're in hell. Stuck on the surface of history. You and I in hell, together forever. Trapped in the present until it's too late. It stays red for 3 days without end. I can't even think of leaving the mountain after 5 weeks away in climate exile. Fire season feels like forever now. I know this book is only an artifact of the real lifelong work in process; the red days are just a precursor to the future beyond this animate bag of language and time, always waiting for what comes next.

Dear Diego,

Sometimes, waiting to hear back from a potential job feels a lot like waiting around to die, or hear word from a test that determines your level of suffering in the world. It reminds me of being young and hearing the words, "we have to talk later." From my parents, always using my anxiety against me and letting me torture myself with the blades of time and anticipation. I remember waiting to talk in my bedroom, shared with my brother, who was outside playing at the time. My parents walked in and dropped a love letter I'd written on my desk or drawers. I can remember which love. Which letter. What lyrics covered the folded square of honesty. They said: *Who's* ██*? You know we'll love you no matter who you love right?* That was what they said together. Alone, my then-father would speak in fists and flexed wrists, wringing my neck in the garage, attempting to beat the faggot out of me in the kitchen or yard. He would always tell me, "God always gives us tests. And you are my test. You are a test that I will not fail." He would pick the fights; he would set the rules. *Keep your hands down. Don't try to save that pretty face.* He'd fuck me up until I was old enough to fight back. Never taller than him. When my lip would quiver like a dog giving warning. My eye still has a twitch. I remember when I snapped and started fighting back. I never heard the word faggot again after that. There was no more sudden fist to the mouth, loud *he's mad you'd better brace yourself* moments. There was a quiet hidden inside me. I think often of the time before that moment, when I understood love without language or pronoun. A joy made entirely of light. This is how I still see love now. Without gender or language, our love is always glowing; always growing beyond the empire's hydra edifice of heteronormative deficits. I spent years gathering words to understand myself. I am still gathering a language with which I hope to adorn the vast and eternal interior comprised of light. All the loves I've fawned over and telephoned and kissed now buried in the soft of my ribs, where their love reverses my bruises, kisses my cuts clean, in a park we built beside a lake, drenched in the heat of valley memories. I was always afraid of everything and learned from fear that feelings should be made secret; bringing one's own truth to light resulted in blood, in bruised and humiliated hurt. I don't know how else to explain it. He beat me until I was ashamed for feeling. Belt vs. Psyche. I was made to feel a constant estrangement from my truth. I see now that it was this knowing myself so fully that scared his machismo-addled-brain. My truth was a threat to his cycle of wretchedness. So I buried them in the attic of the auditorium where there was a mattress beside the marquee; I hid them in underground bars beside the spine of the continent; on the couch while my parents were out; in actions and riots; work vans and strange houses; I hid them in crystal grids and birds; I hid them hopping walls wearing thick eyeliner; I hid them playing skin games; rainbow parties, and sky high dens of spit and sun. I hid them in the garden of his skin. In the way you held my neck like a daffodil. I didn't have to fight you, or anyone for anything; everything can be heaven once we let ourselves

Love,
un angel.

Dear Diego,

It's hard to understand much else when weighed down by a
constant temporal paralysis, left weightless and accounted for
down to the key strokes until you're 5 p.m. no sun, all anxiety
about the next thing, the next day, and how will you make it
to the weekend anyway? You don't understand that the life of a
poet is not glamorous. The suffering that brings the language
raining down night can come from living, or working to live;
to suffer, to write. Transfigure the suffering into something
useful. Something I've learned in trying to stay alive is surren-
dering to what's happening around you when you feel like it's
officially become too much, if only for a moment. You make a
wave to ride or dive under; there is no drowning here. You're
always here for you. At the end of the day, you're still going to
be there. We write poetry because the body can only hold so
much. The body can only hide so much. The body can only
heal so much. Hurt so much. Oftentimes we expel the devas-
tation without really knowing it. The ruin reverses back into a
reflection of sky. We write poetry because time does not heal
all wounds. Sometimes, we need sound to accompany that.
Sometimes, we need a prayer, or a song to help us continue on
through it. We are ultimately mortal beings. Our time is not
meant for warfare. Nor is it just for sitting there and letting di-
saster overtake us. We are resilient insofar as we are feeling. We
know that we are alive, even as we read or hear this. We know
the lungs function long enough to give purpose to the motion
propelling them; the larynx there, too, giving moon to tongue
and light to breath. The dream has gotten a little louder now,
by the time you get to this. The body alight with remembrance
of past lives. We write poetry because we remember what it's
like to die. We remember what it's like to live beyond other

parts of ourselves. We know the pain of continuing beyond the best of you. You write poetry because keeping yourself alive isn't all of it. We continue despite the constant Machiavellian charade of society; we continue beyond the draconian doubts of the haters, cause. See, we are star-fire. The kind of light that presses on for ten thousand years and more, beyond the sound of the end. Our energy is the epilogue of empires.

Dear Diego,

I dreamt I drank my lepidolite with its pink tourmaline—like licking sand on the ocean's shore/floor—the lepidolite pulped upon my tongue like wet sand and I ate it. Columns of tourmaline pink and crunching in the pocket of mouth.

I am become the charcoal peony flooded with ands—do I die before they eat me to bloom—to be consumed by the fire of light; to wilt a language in the sun.

Ants swarm the peony; consumption in search of sun; how do we bring the flowers back?

Dear Diego,

My mouth sprouts mimosa flowers and I begin vomiting acres of rain. I get so sick when I enter language without my body. All my talismans of self crumble under the weight of whiteness which demands acquiescence; the colonizers require you to colonize too and be colonized over and over and over again until you forget how to pronounce your name. When I try to pronounce my name, my mouth pours volcanos of acid rain transforming these oppressive monuments and mushmouths into earthen materials again. I vomit Pyrocumulus clouds across the continent in search of my name. Waging migraine auras against reality, trying to be free of this Western way of seeing. Every doctor I've ever seen tells me that I don't actually understand my pain. Ibuprofen again. Co-pay again. We don't want you endangering the community with a sense of liberation; who knows what you would do with actual relief. You might learn to be free of the constant pain. You might demand to be free of all suffering. You might put 2 & 2 together and realize the colonies and your pain are 4 nothing more than the expansion of misery so that the ruling class can hop on rocket ships while they wither our planet into oblivion. You might figure out how to pronounce yourself clearly. We need you to say "debt" debt debt debt debt debt. We need you to say this so that billionaires can unbuckle their seatbelts in space for 4 minutes of weightlessness. It's just like Gil Scott-Heron said, "I can't pay no doctor bill (but Whitey's on the moon)"

-A pile of unsent letters.

DEAR DIEGO,

DON'T MIND THE BLOOD BY THE DOOR
I'VE JUST BEEN WRITING ALL DAY
DON'T MIND THE WAY I KEEP PACING ON THE CEILING
I JUST KEEP CRYING FOREVER
DON'T MIND THE LONG NIGHTS THAT BECOME DAYS
THIS IS ALWAYS BECOMING
DON'T MIND THE BLOOD ON THE WALLS
I JUST KEEP TRYING TO THINK
DON'T MIND THE WAY I KEEP RETCHING UP NOTH-
ING JUST TRYING TO POEM
DON'T MIND THE LONG WAY
I HEAR IT'S THE SCENIC ROUTE WE LIKE THE FIRE
DON'T MIND THE BLOOD AROUND MY MOUTH
I'M A VEGETARIAN THIS IS HUMAN
DON'T MIND THE WAY I KEEP DIGGING UP YOUR
CORPSE I'M JUST CODEPENDENT AND COPING
DON'T MIND THE BLOOD I'VE BEEN
TRYING TO TRANSLATE I'M SURE IT'LL DRY SOON
DON'T MIND THE WAY I KEEP WASHING MY HANDS
WITH MY TEARS IT'S ORGANIC
DON'T MIND THE LONG WINDED LETTERS I'VE SENT
YOU FOR YEARS & YEARS IDK IF U READ
DON'T MIND THE BLOOD I KEEP POURING INTO MY
COFFEE I'VE MOVED ON FROM ROSES
DON'T MIND THE WAY I KEEP RETURNING TO THE
SCENE OF OUR SOURCE, IT'S NOT IRL
DON'T MIND THE LONG MOTIONS OF LIVING
WE'RE BOTH DEAD AT THE SAME TIME EVENTUALLY
DON'T MIND THE BLOOD I SPILLED FROM MY FACE
I HEAR I LOOK HEALTHIER THESE DAYS

DON'T MIND THE WAY I KEEP YOUR NAME IN MY
HEAD LIKE A DEER TICK, BULLSEYE
DON'T MIND THE LONG GONE ASPECTS OF MY
CULTURE YOU BURNT US INTO THE SKY

Dear Diego,

Did I ever tell you that I, too, live betwixt two streams when it rains? I smile at the small similarities in a bashful shame of having written you all these love letters for all these years. What are we to one another? Would you care if you knew I was writing to you all these years later? 455 years is a long time, Diego. Long enough to see the oppressor's empire fall and rebuild and fall and become other empires that fall. Long enough to see every one of those so-called explorers dead. What am I become to myself? Who am I all these years later? Tato's mother calls it "colonial sickness," the latent radiation poisoning of colonization. I call it colonial atrophy. I can almost feel the atoms falling off of me. Five thousand at a time. Cells regenerating every seven years while their atoms phase in and out of existence. Between realities is where I write to you. Live from the mystery itself, writing love letters to keep myself alive.

Dear Diego,

I can't draw you. To be fair, I've never tried. I find that when I attempt a line, it turns violent. As if my body rejects the notion of soft, delicate capture. Instead, you emerge from the rubble, in the aftermath of ruin; you resemble regurgitated molecules forcibly removed from their decomposition in time to illuminate the concepts that came before. Before concept existed the actual. The "real" cannot exist in this social economy. It has no "likable" value.

The gaze chained to critique—

                    The blood stained to teeth—

The miles brazed to feet—

Diego,

Diego,

I was trying

I dreamt of a glass entryway:
I kept cutting myself every
Time I tried to pass through

Diego,

Do you hear that echo? The way we
touch each other's reverberations to
shatter the glass scrim of reality that
has betwixt us into two sides of a

Diego,
Diego,

Do you hear that echo? The way we
touch each other's reverberations to
shatter the glass scrim of reality that
has betwixt us into two sides of a
cloud

I dream of a glass entryway:
I keep cutting myself every
Time I try to pass through

Diego,   cloud

Do you hear that echo? The way we
touch each other's reverberations to
shatter the glass scrim of reality that
has betwixt us into two sides of a

Diego,

You and I are everwhere and
everything all at once: a diamond
mind electron probability bath –
we happen at the same time
atoms tangling into a braid of

Dear Diego,

I want you to imagine a gray sky.

I want you to imagine a gray   Now puncture it.
sky

What escapes?

What's revealed when we make space for what we don't know?

What becomes lost when we are forgiven? What learns to grow?

Sometimes, I get way too high to hear you, Diego.

Imagine the vacuum of space with its ancient little freckles made of more light than I'll ever know up close. We are made of light & time, Diego. Who do we experience when we are by ourselves? Will I ever figure it out?

Dear Diego,

I
am
I will,
I am; I will
I am; I will; I am
I will; I am; I will; I am
I will; I am; I will I am; I will
I am; I will; I am; I will I am; I will
I am; I will; I am; I will I am; I will I am

I   I
am   am
I will,   I will,
I am; I will; I am   I am; I will; I am
I am; I will; I am; I will I am   I will; I am; I will I am

I am; I will; I am; I will I am; I will I am
I will; I am; I will; I am; I will I am; I will
I will; I am; I will I am; I will
I am; I will; I am
I will,
am
I

90

Dear Diego,

I
will
I will; I
I will; I am.
I will; I am. I will; I am.
I will; I am. I will; I am. I will; I am.
I will; I am. I will; I am. I will; I am. I will; I am.
I will; I am. I will; I am. I will; I am. I will; I am. I will; I am.
I will; I am. I will; I am. I will; I am. I will; I am. I will; I am. I will; I am.
I will; I am. I will; I am. I will; I am. I will; I am. I will; I am. I will; I am. I will; I am.

I
will
I will; I
I will; I am.
I will; I am. I will; I am.
I will; I am. I will; I am.
I will; I am.
I will; I
will
I

I will; I am. I will; I am. I will; I am. I will; I am. I will; I am. I will; I am. I will; I am.
I will; I am. I will; I am. I will; I am. I will; I am. I will; I am. I will; I am.
I will; I am. I will; I am. I will; I am. I will; I am. I will; I am.
I will; I am. I will; I am. I will; I am. I will; I am.
I will; I am. I will; I am. I will; I am.
I will; I am. I will; I am.
I will; I am.
I will; I
will
I

Dear Diego,

I keep hurting myself trying to understand truth. I keep smashing this continent against my blood and nothing sticks. I keep smashing this mezcla body against the country; returning phantom limbed and in debt. I keep smashing all these dead white names into my skin and still I can't win over my oppressors. I song and dance and die and still I am remembered as a monster. So I stay monstrous. I keep eating prophets. I keep eating stars. I keep eating earthquakes and still they want the human in me. Not realizing they never made a language for me. They looked to animals and beasts and I am all thumbs and teeth and these left feet seek to stomp out white supremacy.

Why are we even talking? These fascists need burying. There are fruit trees I've yet to plant. There's still a third act to be had. The woods shall move upon the state and the oligarchs shall be splayed. There will be no king left in kingdom. There will be a planet or there will be nothing.

There will be nothing. There will be nothing. There will be nothing.

Dear Diego,

On the far side of knowledge is unknowing and intuition and I often dream of your sweat pressed against my own as we turn into ashes in the fire you started. I realized the spiral was not solid matter but variant frequency; we catch sight of each others harmonics in the passing void y every Tun keeps turning as our solar system corkscrews its way in an easy oblivion. Diego, I wasn't ever supposed to love you and here we are all these letters later my dear Scorpio, we wheeze asthmatic in the key of C and our octaves rub together like embers above the platform in Maní Yucatán and it's 1562 pressed upon 2022 and so forth and so on and it's your corpse that keeps me warm; they never really buried you, did you know that? You are not a destination and cannot be. Diego, you are like this natural spring I came upon while hiking. You are another form of atom bomb, and I am only the sky y todo lo que quiero es lluvia lluvia lluvia.

Tu amor,
A

Dear Diego,

I don't want to talk about you anymore.
It's so wearing to have to bring you up over and over and over again—I'm so tired. What it is about you that keeps me curious? You know, it's still crazy to me that your actual crime when standing trial against the crown of spain was for utilizing inquisitional tactics without the consent of the crown. Not the atrocity itself, but the lack of permission from the governing empire to commit these acts of atrocity. As with any empire (even now) there must be paperwork. Paperwork and paid respects and proper channels and pious men. I think that toxic masculinity is the death of all things—the need to spread seed and "discover" and kill and destroy and manifest white destiny—to erase one name and stain another over it. I always think about this when I learn the names of flowers and trees and shrubs and I can't help but wonder what they were before all this blood and agony. What did it mean to name yourself? What did it mean to negotiate one's own mother tongue, to create new meaning out of spectral sounds—wil I ever learn to say, "I forgive you"?

Do I even have to?
I don't think I do.

I don't think I will.
I love you still,

-Tu angelitx

94

Dear Diego,

What is there to even say anymore—what is time? What does it mean to be alive? Are you and I still tethered together by our double helix heart strings? Which of us is vestigial? Do you still weep when I weep? Do you sleep when I sleep? Sometimes, I think you're the microclimate where I live. A Steller's Jay screaming its head off. Sometimes, I think you're in the microclimate where I live. A Steller's Jay screaming its head off, hopping tree to tree in search of unattended nests with eggs to prey upon. Sometimes, I think you're the wild grey luminescence that emerges in the early mornings when the mountain is more of a cloud than a mountain. When the strange loom of dreams is still woven to the waking wash of awareness. How far could your hauntings possibly carry you through time and space—the energies of your memory and name being spoken or read or written reinvigorating your consciousness from the ink-black oblivion you wound up in. Two woodpeckers are outside in the pine, their bright red heads streaking across the mist like twin comets. Your last words were something about your enemies all around you closing in. You insisted on wearing your robes—you couldn't be without the habit. Your armor of wretchedness. I have to squabble with white men about who you really are—who I really am. Nobody believes me. The colonizers constantly scream at me to balance their histories and shortcomings on my head while walking a spiral of barbed wire. They scream at me to only know myself through their eyes—that dead glazed gaze of the colonizer-industrial complex. They scream at us to balance their traumas and atrocities. They scream at us to educate them and understand where they're coming from as they bleed the land and our psyches dry. They paint their faces and take back the scraps they so generously offered us by way of grants and scholarships. They scream at us to accept their freedoms. They scream until I can't hear anything but my own heartbeat and breathing. I don't have a discovery channel production budget. I'm not National Geographic. A Steller's Jay lands upon the giant sequoia outside my window. Those black eyes staring holes into mine. I know it's you. Writing may take many forms. Sometimes, it's a letter; sometimes, it's a Steller's Jay screaming, chased off by a woodpecker. How do I chase away your ghost from the echoes of history? How does one tune such an organism as time? How can we get the ledger to sing of what really happened? What really happened? How can there be such malice and hatred within the dark heart of man? I don't understand it. I just don't understand. Such wickedness veiled by a flimsy language. A series of dictionaries burying tongues that struggle to feel the sun again. How many words will it take to set the ledger straight? How many more years? How many more letters? How long must we wait? As I type this, I know that the time for waiting is a long gone ruse of the ruling class. I know that I'll write a billion letters and even more words, I'll use my body till it withers. I don't even care if I don't see it in my lifetime. Diego, the clouds are coming down again to water the peach tree in a gentle mist. The pine is growing pale glowing neon pinecones. The hawthorn tree is sighing. The woodpecker flies. All I know is you did your best to make us die. You tried to erase everything behind me. And here I am writing these endless love letters to a dead demon. A genocidal monster wearing the veil of a lone pale god. A coward in a cloak collapsing into my arms, centuries later.

Love,
A

Dear Diego,

I don't know that I can defeat you. I don't know that I can win. I don't know that I'll live to see the other side of the dream in my head. I don't know if it matters. These brief glimpses of a futurity beyond the scar tissue in the sky. I keep scrying clouds and leaves after it rains. I keep screening the energies I allocate from myself and the rest of the world. I keep tightening the circle until all I'm left with is your heart in my palms, my heart in my heart; our hearts superimposed upon one another—I pump blood from your dust; your darkness lends me its shadow to wear like a cloak. I keep shedding these toxic husks of love and emptiness when I write to you—like coming out of my skin, coming down from interdimensional dissolution and time travel. Sometimes, I'd like to think we knew one another when you were breathing. Maybe that's why I can't let you go, all these lifetimes later, I'm haunted by your scraps and stains. I keep rubbing the pieces of you that reside in me like the friction will evacuate you from my body. Like decolonization is even possible. Like colonization isn't a constant echoing dog whistle attempting to erase the frequencies of our ancestors from our memory banks. That's the problem with history: all this, *told by an idiot. A tale full of sound and fury, signifying nothing.* All this mess and mess and mess and mess and no clean up. I keep trying to scoop and save the salt of my family. Trying to make a menagerie of our histories and ancestor's histories and I keep forgetting my own to keep making room for what's already been taken from us. I keep practicing a kind of silence that doesn't end. I keep trying to clear my mind of Time. I keep trying to access the Akashik records and travel through the spiral to find you so that maybe we can think through this together and remember. Do you remember everything? Do you remember anything at all? I hold the husk of the dying empire to my dry skin like pumice to callus. I keep trying to wash my hands of your hands. The way those hands took everything and accomplished nothing. I am not afraid of you, Diego. I am not afraid of the echoes that find me in the dark, the sudden thump of your ghost at 3 a.m. asking me again to write again.

I can't keep vomiting all this language back into my blood. I can't keep using (y)our heart as a coping mechanism, nibbling on the dark flesh of what connects us. I keep thinking there might be a healing narrative at work here, where, if only… and yet I know this is a lie, just like your sympathetic-to-the-colonizer history. Maybe feeling better is not what we want. No. I want to remember. I want to remember every loss. I want to remember how, despite the hoards of white history, we remain. We continue to bloom for no one but us. Until we are once again the sky.

A

Dear Diego,

I keep writing these broken pyramids, cracked open and ver-
tical, separated by language, sometimes a single word or let-
ter—an idea can be enough to levitate a whole civilization,
capable of crumbling the golden cow of capital and state in a
single sentence. The leaves are falling early this year, still sum-
mer and yet the sighing continues. Sometimes, it's termites
taking down the trees. Sometimes, it's just time. I never think
of trees as having any kind of set death. Every tree I see, I as-
sume, will outlast me. Every tree I see is older than I'll ever be.
That's the way I treat most trees, aware of the scale at which
they live their lives, their language of earth and atmosphere.
I wonder about the myths that trees make and what culture
might mean to the images of eyes that emerge from the bark of
the birch. I wonder about the language between things and if
that language acts as matter acts, in a kind of iridescent repul-
sion of electrons, the absences simulating the "touch" between
things. Sometimes, I think about the touch between us. Read-
er and Writer; correspondent and corresponded, the speed at
which our electrons rush to reach each other—an electricity
that emits itself beyond corporeal time. The time of these an-
cient trees. Brahmin's taking whole centuries to form a single
thought. The turn of the clock. Another season gone. Follow-
ing the listening limbs, how the fingers fidget across the robot
to unlock a set of learned language. I wander through trace,
casting out flares of poetry and memory, these glowing things
that mean things to me. I'm more interested in sentiment and
sincerity than I am in meaning or winning. What's it mean to
feel, and I mean really feel, your feelings? How is it that you
are alive? How have you survived to where you are now? How
have you grown into another organism and do you still use

your roots? Have you learned to become interplanetary? Have you bathed in the wash of the sea? Have you seen the spine of the continent? Have you made something for someone? Are you still learning to be free? There are so many molecules in the sky right now. Reach out and touch another now. Learn to listen to the threads of time—how they shimmer and vibrate beyond our corporeal selves. How larger bodies of time absorb energy; how our energy is finite and must be directed towards a sky of our own making. Sometimes, the surrounding trees tell me things. Sometimes, we wake up early to visit the ocean and it reminds me that I am nothing. This life a bubble on a wave on a shore I'll never fully comprehend. And still we learn to read the wind. Learn to thread the centuries through a song. Carried away by what comes next.

Dear Diego,

Tell me what you know of stars. Tell me what you know of living. Tell me what you believe in your heart to be truth. Do you still think about us when you're lonely? Do you know what it means to be lonely in every language you speak? Do you know what it means to be lonely in tongues that have vanished or been burned away before you could speak? Do you know how many conquistadors it takes to ruin my day? Do you know how many bibles I've owned and lost and kept and thrown out? Do you know how many churches and citadels I've wept and pissed in? Do you know how many I've seen baptized? Do you know how many prayers I speak? Do you know what it is you've done to me? Tell me what you know of departure. Tell me what you know of ruin. Tell me what you really mean. Do you know how many times have passed since your time? Do you know how many colonizers it takes to ruin my day? Do you know how many have died? Do you know how to get to heaven? Do you know the road to El Dorado? Do you have any change? Do you even have a chance? Do you speak amerikkkan? Do you hide your heart like a reef? Do you dream of many dreams? Do you recognize the pain in my childhood screams? Do you want to be the parent? Do you want to hold these shuddering shoulders until the earthquake hits? Do you know how to save a life? Do you know how to write? Do you know what time it is? Do you know how to come back home? Do you know what this is anymore? Tell me the truth. Tell me everything about you. Tell me why you did it. Tell me why you didn't. Tell me everything. Do you remember? Do you think about the downfall? Do you think about the darkness? Do you think about the blood? Do you think about the sun? Do you think about the ripples across reality? Do you think about the way out? Do you think about my eyes? Do you think about the sky? Do you think about the violence? Do you think about the heat? Do you think about the boat? Do you think about the screams? Do you think about the lies? Do you think about the water? Do you dream about me? Do you even care? Do you want to make it better? Do you want to make it out alive? Do you want to be alive? Do you care if I die? Do you care if we all die? Do you? Tell me what you know about the end. Tell me what you know about oblivion. Tell me what you know about the truth beyond you. Tell me what you know of moons. Tell me you love me.

Please.

Diego,

I only dream of learning to pronounce myself clearly.

Dear Diego,

Some days, the call of the void is stronger than others. I am so afraid of living sometimes. Always in the unknown muck of it—too much to plaster language to. I could spend one million years thinking about this mountain. It would take every dictionary in every language to explain the sea, and even then we wouldn't know it. Knowing is nothing. Everything is nothing. Language only places more space between the thing and what it is instead of addressing the thing for what it actually is. Language is a tricky fox, agent of chaos; history is a whirlpool of white words insisting on being learned as "fact" and "actual" and "right." Sometimes, I try to undress the words that cover my body. Sometimes, I try and name the histories that engulf me, histories I emanate without knowing. Sometimes, I try to untangle the violence inside me. A chorus of beasts seeking a kind of supremacy, not understanding that word, supremacy, is a false identity. How can you pour all your being into the sense that you are more than the moon itself? How could anyone believe that they reign supreme over the sea? How could anyone think themselves as not being enmeshed in the mud, blood, and ectoplasm of the planet? My veins are braided into the back of your neck, Diego—our hair woven together to form a hydra that emerges from my neck in the form of a mouth. I spew the braided tongues of colonization. I Godzilla the colonies into a flattened disc that becomes a cloud. I keep chewing your life in my mouth. I keep swallowing little bits of your clothing, coughing up the blood of my ancestors. My body keeps leaking blood when I least expect it and I am less afraid of death than I am of forgetting. How do you hang onto a memory beyond the veil? Is there such a thing? Must I stack these stones of language in hopes they last a set of centuries.

The way the pyramids became mountains. The ways in which the Maya held onto who they used to be in the face of the struggling sun that called itself conquistador and who said, "burn the boats."

Dear Diego,

I wake up with the sun to eat the resinous scroll of unending glimpses and refractive visions into the dark heart of humanity. I wake up and try to eat my own heart to save it from the disappointment to come. The disappointment it seeks in these timelines, all touch and go, never considering the lingering residue of what I can only describe as evil. How it braids itself into your hair, infecting your thoughts, reminding you of those who would rather choose oblivion than compromise. I keep watching these druids cull demons from the ignorant—keep seeing these awful corners of humanism that lack a sense of goodness; they're selfish and what's worse, they don't care. I keep breaking off shards of their momentary exorcisms and summonings while scrolling—I keep these awful things to remember. To remind me. So that I don't get caught up in toxic positivity. I don't want to get caught up in the trappings of hope. Been there done that. My grandmother tells que soy pessemista y yo digo que no es cierto soy realista. I am always on a quest for the real. The actual. The truth. Getting to the bottom of it. I keep returning to this sense of the "dark heart of man"—Conrad's heart of darkness, Kurtz in jungle screaming with fire all around. I think some people think of Kurtz as the hero of the story. I think some people think only white people write stories. They keep the mirrors we need hidden from us until we learn to see ourselves in the face of our oppressor, the face of the colonizer. The face of the "nation" country, or state. They being the ruling class. They being the state itself. They being army of Kurtz fuckers that would rather rule over rape & murder rather than allow everyone to have something eat. Seems to me there's this wide-ranging distortion to history cemented in the subjective experience of history's many afterlives. I keep shirking off the shadow of everything that came before me so that I might see what comes next or, put it another way: I want to understand the thing in itself. I know the Maya weren't saints. I know toxic masculinity is the death of all things. I know colonization is neither the alpha nor omega. I know there is more. That's why I keep trying to read the sky every morning, asking the clouds to tell me something about the future. Seeing what can be gleaned of the histories those clouds contain. How the water retains memory—how the clouds you see are older than *the last syllable of recorded time*. What is it they're saying? What is it they're remembering? How far along the spiral are we anyway? Who's really been writing to who? *Out, out brief candle.* Life is but a walking shadow. *A poor player that struts and frets his hour upon the stage and then is heard no more.*

Dear Diego,

I want revenge. I don't know how else to put it. I don't want
anything back. I want something new. A newness from the
ruin. I desire the death of my enemies. Enemies like the war
of the '80s. The '90s; the housing market crash; the banks.
The bankers. The war itself. I keep telling people that I know
I won't see these empires of capitalism and white supremacy
crumble in my lifetime, but in the dead of night I keep writing
these little flower pots plump with bombs of luminous mem-
ory; I try and connect other wires across the synapse seeking
out the alleyway escape. Over the wall in one motion. Fifity
cinder blocks high. I keep trying to imbue these poems with
schematics of a different future. I keep trying to explain that
bricks bounce, but with enough force, a cinder block won't.
Sugar in the gas tank to break their transit down. I'll be honest
with you, Diego. I want more than just revenge. I understand
revenge is just one elemental dimension to what comes next;
I know that ultimately there are things more important than
revenge. Like, liberation. Education as a form of liberation. It's
more than knowing how to use a tool or two. It's the whole bag.
It's a constant exchanging of tools. It's a constant reassessment
and recalibration of yourself and your tools. It's understand-
ing that you can be wrong. It's knowing that ultimately you are
both insignificant and the whole entire world, all at once. It's
more than just you. Liberation is a constant process. Libera-
tion is a perpetual trial and error. It's not any one thing. There
is no end point. And maybe that's the point. There is no point
at which a thing ends necessarily. It's a matter of how that thing
is dealt with and discussed. I will never write enough letters or
poems to cure the world of its ailments, and still I write. Still
I remember. Still I choose to work against the face of constant

death. This empire of misery and dust. I know that I am but one pen. One poet. One person. One one. And yet. I contain multitudes. I am every highway I've ever wandered, weary or wired; I am the ten thousand hours and then some; I am the aching mountain of haunted earth. I am the architectures of cellular memory, the overly antsy, the sick with feelings; I am an ocean of now. I can't help but throw this whole body of flesh and language at the threshold of history and all temporality. I have to try. I have to try. I have to try. I've got to. All I have ever wanted was to be alive. And then I learned that it's more than that. I, idiot-tongued manifestation of reckoning, named after a song, self-made seraphim of the middle passage, marred by the many manifestations of living in this reality of thought and matter and wave. Living beyond the revenge. Living long enough to see one's enemies fall. That's the real dream. Narrating the remembering. Recording the recall. Sealing the synapse. Understanding the subjectivity and not being swayed by it. Staying with the endless madness of the mess. Staying mad. Remaining vigilant. Until everyone is free.

Dear Diego,

Sometimes, writing to you feels like drinking gasoline from the pump —the sound of liquefied time dripping in the moonlight. A hundred thousand fossils pouring out of my mouth and into my organs. I get so thirsty writing to you, Diego. I find myself craving freeway rain with a thumb on the dotted line home. Sometimes, I pine for the guardrail to give way. The call of the void. L'appel du vide. Do you still feel this? Did you ever? The fleeting thought of oblivion? I always arrive at the cusp of destruction with you, Diego. I never know just how far to go, or if such a thing even exists. This notion that if I destroy you thru erasure, if I could rewrite a history, am I anything other than what you are? If I set fire to your robes, if I robbed the Iberians of their histories, if I replaced every colonizer and colony with new words. I don't think there is enough language to do what you thought you did by burning everything away. I don't think humans have a real grasp on scale, everything in our lives is inevitably short-term in relation to the life of the planet we exist on. You really thought you could "save" us. You really thought you could just rob, rape, torture, and murder us. You thought you could burn the bodies of our ancestors. You thought you could tie our wrists behind our backs, hoisted up by the language of your "god," to paint boiling pig's fat on bare flesh to…what? Get the demons out? To get to the truth? You would use these inquisitional tactics to demand information that did not exist. Do you know how many recanted their confessions after their blood had coagulated and covered their wounds? Do you know how far some had to travel to find idols in ruins just to appease your fantasies of heresy and demonology? Your imagination was more evil than anything my ancestors admitted to. That's it isn't it? The colonial imagination. That's what's so ruinous and constantly rotting. The last zombie in a world overtaken by flowers, still hungry for something to colonize, something to harm and infect and spread to. A decrepit drooling husk of itself. A caricature of a caricature drawn from drunk memory. Drunk off pig blood riding horses on the beaches of Tulum. Sweating into our sacred waters, unbathed and in agony from the sun. The idea hangs on, glamorized in minds of neocolonizers who claim nationhood and supremacy. The zombie of colonization speaks through them thinking itself alive. Thinking it's still a way of life. To acquiesce and demonize and destroy. I have a dream in which the flowers and vines overtake the zombie of the colonies. I have a dream in which we plant strangler figs in the doors of every oppressor. I have a dream where we don't just "win." That notion exists within the imagination of the colonizer. Within the body of the zombie colonies that continue to repeat the same droning drivel, hungry for subjugate bodies to press the dark fossil of their hearts upon. I would love for you to become my gasoline, Diego. I would love to put every colony in the rearview mirror. I would love to get away from everything and yet. I'm here. Constantly fighting with this invisible zombie. Constantly breaking the fourth and fifth and sixth walls of colonization. Constantly checking myself and my beliefs and the ways in which I carry myself in this world. Constantly trekking the vast deference of my heart, which is also your heart, Diego. I too am zombie. I only want to plant flowers. I don't want to spread the virus I've inherited. I want to understand it. I want to not just eliminate it but learn from it. I want to plant flowers. I want to plant a garden of roses, like my grandfather Xix before me. I want to build a beautiful line of bricks as my grandfather Jose once laid. I want to feel the sun on my skin. I want to feel air that lies beyond colonization. I can almost taste it, Diego. Can you taste it too? There is water there.

Maybe a Dzonot.

-a

Dear Diego,

Do you know the fable of the scorpion and the frog? Have you ever heard that one or were fables only for blasphemers & heretics? I wonder what you thought about writing. How you thought about writing and language and surely you wrote more than the facsimile notes that survived you. I wonder if you wrote poems. Do scorpions write poems? I don't mean Scorpio's, though, if memory serves, you and I are tied to one another by blood and planets and time's heavy breathing. Both of us asthmatic and stricken with an urge to leave our origins. You took a boat. And I by bus, train, plane, and car. You were born two days after me; we missed each other by 465 years and some 5,800 miles, triangulated by our Yucatecan tethering. Sometimes, I think I see you in the mirror, like there might be a map to you in the optical calcite specimens that find me. Like, if I could just hone in on the electrons between us, if I could obtain the spin of your atoms, we might know one another. We might be able to move forward. Together, without having to kill one another. You who were born between two streams and I, a Los Angeles accident, always in a hurry to leave. I wonder which of us is the scorpion in this story. I wonder if people think about who the scorpion in their life is. I wonder how many amerikkkans think they're the frog. How many make up the myth of an invisible scorpion, wide as a noun, to take the place of that which keeps them from obtaining their crown of capital, that which prevents their ability to become billionaires. The real scorpion is colonization. The real scorpion is white supremacy. The real scorpion is capitalism. The real scorpion is pride. The real scorpion is the system of systems that perpetuates this death cult of capital until we are buried by symbols.

Dear Diego,

It seems I can't escape the violence of whiteness, even in my dreams. This morning I woke up suddenly at 6 a.m.; the rain stopped and a cloud consumed the tract of land, tracing the microclimate around me. I was at a Valley party. Specifically, 818. We were in the backyard, cups in hand, trying to relax. Trying hard to catch the specificity of the fragment before the memory dissipates into my cup of coffee. I get distracted by the language on the screen/the language on my to-do list; the language in my head. Your fingers in my mouth while I try to pronounce myself at the counter. The constant onslaught of communication and understanding. Some mornings I wonder what it must be to become a tree, to learn the language of oxygen and empathy. Dreams have been few and far between during these last four years. When they have emerged, they've strung together these bits of energy into a floating fishing village off the continent of my memory/in the planet of my body, I retreat from language and become image and action, paper and water; sound and color. It upsets me to think I can't be safe in my dreams. I think a lot of things about dreams. I know some people think that you are everything in your dreams, the space, the people, the words; it's all you, and to a certain extent I think that's true. But, I also think there's something to be said about the visions that come through unexpectedly—other energies intersecting, colliding, and transmitting from beyond this plane of existence. When I see the dead in my dreams I know I am not them. I carry them with me in my body, where they continue to wander in search of other afterlives beyond the flesh. I try and listen to them when they speak. Most often the dead are deeply quiet. They smile with their eyes. They have the ability to grow older than the day they died. They have other work to do where they are now. When I have felt my most in the ground they have come to me. I wonder if the dead ever visited you, or if they do now. What do we make of these energies existing so far out beyond the body? What do we do with the things we learn from dreams? Last night this dream took me by surprise. There I was, somewhere between second and third person perspective in the dirty backyard of an 818 house conglomerate. It was like our family home had sunk into another death beyond the one it had. Strangers all around. The familiarity of a red cup in hand. I think we were all trying to relax. That's when this proud boy baby-faced buzz cut stocky white boy started making a ruckus in the house no one owned. Incendiary and pink about the face, the wasted white boy came out trying to fight everyone around him. Threatening to kill us all. The threat of whiteness now so pervasive that it's found its way into my subconscious. The threat of constant whiteness now so viral it's found a way to astral project. The proud boy project of intercepting the dreams and resting hours of every non-white person around them. On that astral scam. The cosmic caucasity of it all. You know, even in my dream I didn't feel like fighting. I'm so tired. I walked to the trunk of a car and grabbed a tire iron. Tried to talk to the bull in the panaderia down. Tried to de-escalate the constant onslaught of death that whiteness exudes. Tried to put that candle out. Hate the plastic vanilla stench trying to cover up the bodies in the walls. Our bodies in their gardens. Our bodies building their homes. Our bodies making their foods. Our bodies expiring before their eyes, without a shred of empathy or understanding that we too are human. I looked into that white boy's eyes and saw your eyes, Diego. I saw my own eyes. My father's eyes. The eyes of every man that has ever put hands on me. That had ever harmed me. Choked me. I looked into the eyes of toxic masculinity, directly. I saw nothing I could not overcome. I saw nothing that could defeat me. I saw the whole of history shrinking back down into a shriveled cock across the Atlantic, withering into the echo of ignorance. I saw Fanon's words written across the angry forehead demanding my death, it read, "Decolonization is always a violent phenomenon." Decolonization is not a metaphor. Decolonization is a verb. It is a series of actions aimed at shaking us free from the entropy of whiteness. The constant death cult of machismo. I seek no empathy from my enemy. I no longer seek understanding. Not everyone has to be on the boat. I will burn the boat myself with me aboard if I have to. May this ancestral shadow of colonial death die with me.

Diego,

I write you a codex of blood and coffee; I write you a pile of ashes and stems. I've been growing moldy in my constant reverie of a life lived plainly. A sense of "security" from employment; I still can't save money. Precarity is all around us. Ultimately there is no escaping the precarious, but isn't that something beautiful? I'm really asking because most of me doesn't know how beautiful it is to be in constant turmoil; I don't yet understand the beauty of misery. I've yet to know suffering as anything but that: suffering. I had an interesting talk with the homie the other day, where he brought up the fact that capitalism is built upon a foundation of South and Central American, and African riches and raw materials. Capitalism is built upon a foundation of genocide and forgetting. Literally, the system that perpetuates the suffering of the disenfranchised, marginalized, and otherwise undercommon started from what was stolen. I think I text the plug more than I text my mom, or rather, I see the delivery driver more than I see my own family face to face. What's relevant anymore, Diego? The apocalypse is here, or coming, and I don't know what to do with that information. I don't know what to do with the world ending. I guess I can keep writing to you. Seems there are poems that pop out like mirrors in the sand, reflecting the ocean. I write you water. I write you ocean. I write you war time. I write to resist fascism. So much of my life is a matter of resistance. Though never outright and loud about it, I sustain a resonance, hold a timbre; I can blue with the best of them. Think skin, Diego. The book is skin. Our letters here are scar tissue, building back over the ruptured entity. Think of how we've formed a tract of dzonots y fuego y mi alma está cansado con tanto milagro estoy vivo estoy viva, y mi vida es lleno de

agua y lleno de la escritura, y a veces hay poetas y a veses ay
monstruos y sirenas y vatos y ranflas y lenguas y carne y san-
gre y rosas y oro y sangre y oro y sangre y oro y sangre y oro
y sangre y oro y la vida, mi vida, nuestro vida somos sangre y
cielo somos ";"

XO,
A

Dear Diego,

I will not diminish the fullness of my truth. I think so often there's this flattening or shrinkage of the self to accommodate others. A survival mechanism rooted in colonization. To don a mirror tongue when communication with your would-be/ someday executioner. Exhaustion seems to get the better of me while never leaving the hypothetical. I cycle through the archetypes. Entangle the ephemeral with the ongoing, noting every emergence, calling attention to the patterns. Parsing out notions of scale across these time cones to create the hyper reality of the present moment, ever fleeting. I seek to be the knowledge of your atoms, Diego; I wish to know your every molecule and movement. What are the gestures of this ongoing genocide? What will it take to change the narrative? To adhere a sense of reality to the language. I keep trying to build these models of resistance from within the tongues of my oppressors. Something about the master's tools. Something about amerikkkan assimilation. Something about the way I can't ever seem to feel at home or alright wherever I go. Moving through this ocean of whiteness like cuttlefish made of oil, unable to assimilate. I keep trying to carve out these small enclaves of non-reality in which I can work out what reality really means to me. I have been working so hard at unlearning. Investigating the things my dreams tell me, listening to the threads that tug me towards the future. Terrified of becoming. Still, more terrified of never knowing what I could become. And so I press on with ancestral compass disarming my enemy with language. What I really want is revenge. It will only be perceived as revenge by my enemies. All my kin and me know that revenge is really just becoming. Stretching out across the earth as a new net of clouds, something like a sphere of rainbow chandeliers.

Dear Diego,

Eventually we must all confront our "masters," for there are no masters in reality. In reality there are no super powers. We stop scraping the sky. Everything is horizontal. Forward moving in that there is growth. Everyone eats. Capitalism becomes a bad dream. Eventually we must all confront ourselves. Break everything down into what it amounts to. Who are you really? When no one else is looking, what really matters most to you beyond the materiality of your reality. What would it mean if we were all free of capitalism? What would it mean if we all called in sick. What would the world be if we were actually a we? I believe we could become the weather. I believe we could exceed the language we were given. I believe we could create whole new worlds with more than just words and imagination. We need a little less keyboard a little more I will fight you in the street. A little more confronting the imaginary. A little more light on the dead-eyed demons. A little more wrathful compassion. As in, I will not be providing critical race and ethnic studies sermons for the willfully deaf and damned. As in: no unity with fascists. As in: I do not befriend my murderers and, if I do, may they be haunted by rage, set free of this ragged body. Constantly peeling back this personhood and remembering that I am nothing.

Let the ocean of your mind wash away the mountains of your mind. What remains?

Dear Diego,

You've been with me through flood and fire and fire and flood again. I've written to you more than I've ever written to anyone. Sometimes, I think you are all my dead friends. Sometimes, I think you are one of my ancestors. Sometimes, I think your face is my face both with our own habits. Sometimes, I think of us as two ropes of light, entwined and gathering galaxies, undisturbed in endless space. Sometimes, I think you're my own personal saint. Sometimes, I think I'm cursed. Sometimes, I wonder how much longer I can keep at it. I'm starting to feel my body in new, sore ways. These hands aren't what they used to be. It's getting harder to, well. You don't need to know about that. Sometimes, it feels like you might be my only confidant. I write to you everyday inside my head and it's never mattered if you wrote back. Sometimes, water must move where it wants to go. You know, I think we might be a kind of waterfall. An anomaly where water flows in every direction. Takes flight. Becomes cloud in sky. Sometimes, I think I'll never stop writing to you. I'll never stop writing. This strange dance of language, energy, and time. The way we fold the brain into future shapes. Sometimes, I think we're stuck in this last call, slow dance. Sometimes, I feel Atlas, and still have to clock in, and clock out, and write these emails. Like you're the world and I'm finally starting to feel sore. You're the empire that led the narrative. Sometimes, I think we might be a pair of flowers growing out of a Maya tower with no name, completely swallowed by the gardens of Chaac, without end. Sometimes, I think you and I might be in love. Sometimes, I think you are my family. Sometimes, I hear your voice in the violence of "we" or "our" and sometimes, I say, it's too hard to understand this vast, quantum field of many worlds we call "latinidad." But I'm lying. I'm being lazy. I'm still working on it. I'm busy dissociating into other realities and recall-replays. Drooling poetry stubbornly, trying to sleep with one eye open, outlining this impossible essay that never ends.

Dear Diego,

Some days I wake up angry. Mad mornings. Waking up exhausted and thirsty for more of the same. Constantly engaged in the subtleties of fight and flight, considering the nuances of freeze; watching the rhythms of my heart, listening to the water that makes my body real. I'm always tired because I'm always trying. I'm trying to keep the thing alive. Trying to figure it out. Trying to get to the bottom of Bottom's dream. Trying to get to that in between, or at least attempting to form a language out of it. The adornment of the ineffable. The backdoor to the everything. I'm trying to be here with the busboys of reality, scrubbing the earth like dishes. Trimming the hegemony with guillotines if necessary. Necessity of knowing how to operate a weapon like language. You need to know words mean things. Language is a weapon as much as it is a portal for healing. Sometimes, healing is not what we need. No body is in a hurry to fill the Grand Canyon, or Crater Lake. Sometimes, it's a constant process rather than a concrete end point. Dead car in the redwoods sprouting periwinkles and wild peas. A generational conversation. Vomiting tradition. Vomiting experience as eternal existence and confronting the past with a pistol. No more knife fights. This is a stick up. Sick of the constant surplus of suppression. Sick of the firefight of the white imagination. Sick of the struggling against everything. And still I must. I don't have a choice in the matter. They fucked up letting me live this long. Long enough to think it through. To understand that you and I are together in this. The untangling. The wrestling of the spirits. Trapped in forever fist fight of history and language and energy. I just have to live long enough to die on my own terms, in my own words. *They can't take that away from me...*

Dear Diego,

We finally have it out on the floor of the cosmos, exhausted by the swirl, unable to exhaust without a sense of linear time, we are coexistent with every iteration of the multiverse splintering along each syllable. Learning how the sound haunts the space; how the center haunts the frame. Mischievous little moments keep piling themselves into a certainty where I must confront the ways I have failed to protect that which means most to me. Our time together in these sentences. The way you make me think. We shrink the space/time between us. I'm basically texting you. Hoping you're up and in a space where you can receive this transmission. Trying to transmit the light of the moon; the length of the highway; the heat of the lowlands; the distance from me to you. Within the heart that beats while absorbing these symbols exists a set of multiplexing portals. Hold fast to that present moment that divides this (reality) from that (reality) and let yourself see what's really there, under it. The way the energies of everything you've ever seen or been collect in the dzonot of your life. What portal will you become beyond your mortality? What does it mean that you're my portal to everything, Diego? Is this how you repent? Patron Saint of ancestral oppression? Blessed blasphemous beast of a thousand sins? Burden of burdens. Love of my life. Whatever would I do without you, Diego? I wouldn't exist. I wouldn't be writing this. And you know what? You could keep it. Would gladly trade you two thousand years plus to sleep at the bottom of the Atlantic. Would that none of you survived that first voyage back to Spain. A kraken. A cursed triangle. A rogue pod of mermaids. Anything. And yet you're here. Ignoring my letters. Refusing to be anything but pain, no matter how much you tell me it's love.

Dear Diego,

Sometimes, I can see threads of the future which contain many futures. Sometimes, I see you quite clearly, scared and sweating where you stood. So convinced that the human beings surrounding you were demonic in their difference. So convinced of your mastery of violence and tongues, tortures you called tests. Treacherous is your afterlife, a history rewritten by the supposed "victors" of what? It's still happening isn't it? History continues on in the present moment. The flowers continue beyond their roots. Some become air-plant satellites. Driving forty-eight hours straight with a busted headlight. Right foot made of more than destiny. Heavy like the arc of history. Determined to make sense of our tethering. All binaries are illusions. I know that you and I are colloidal and entwined, woven together to form this rope of time to hoisting up a language out of that which was once redacted.

Dear Diego,

In my dreams we finally find a way to get together and drive to the ocean. We bring everything we need. We discuss the constellations of streetlights and neon signs, the boats and books that create these circuitous archives of association. I teach you to roll a joint and you break the bible down while the waves explain the infinite universe. I show you the ways I've learned to reverse death, or, you teach me how to talk to the living; we write poetry together in these meetings. They happen at the lip of the continent, every night. At the edge of my dreams. Between this body and what lies beyond this place. We dance while oscillating gravity. We make many moons. I play you all these songs I keep writing but can't record. You forgive me for my dark days of sinning and I forgive you for thinking it could be that simple. We talk about healing with you speaking of a wound and a lamb. I try and explain the many wounds of colonization. The ocean punctuates our every sentence with infinity. The inky black midnight melds ocean to heaven as we swig heavy handed from the void. I tell you about the many deaths I've died and my many afterlives. You tell me about the limits of man; the myth of maturity. We talk so long our words start to spill out like sand and the sun never comes up again. We keep drinking from the void. I tell you about how I'm scared of dying, how, deep down, I keep forgetting about my body; how I only see myself in words. You tell me about your lack of body, the empty freedoms of purgatory. We become synonyms for one another. We talk so long lightning strikes twice and we become glass on the last of the coastline. The moon looks upon us polishing our dreams into something resembling a mirror, only more luminous. We talk until the ocean takes the mountains. Until the fire and the flood pass. Until everything grows quiet again. We speak in silence, back and forth, forming a Möbius strip of information: Dharma, back and forth, Dharma, forever exclaiming, expounding, and examining the self of no self, the mirror archive of eternity. The space between us. The time before you set foot on that first boat out of Spain. The time before we both become buried by the sand of our words, all the while adorning the ineffable. This elastic eternity of sound and fury, signifying nothing. A warm and empty nothing. Eventually we talk back and forth so long the ocean begins to sink. We speak with new tongues of water and wave. We keep talking through the mess of masculinities and colonization and keep learning. Eventually, we develop into a language of clouds. Now we learn to rain. We learn the many realities of water. We drift, lonely as a cloud, combining molecules until there is a consciousness alive in the atmosphere, an awareness of learning and relearning—this commitment to sincerity we've always had, it continues to warm the language we're making. We talk so long we invent the word aeon, you add an "s," and I laugh in eternity. We never stop talking long enough to figure anything out. We let the language grow and morph into what's needed. We dream long enough to sleep in the deepest sleeps of dreams and it's there that we finally find each other, Diego. It's there we can rest, in the heart of the process. In the seat of the ongoing, forever learning, untangling, rebraiding, adorning the infinite in a language of our own making. I have a dream where, eventually—

ACKNOWLEDGMENTS

Thank you to my ancestors, my family, my kin, and all who have helped keep me alive.

Thankful for all the cells, cities, selves, and lives I've lived in and been through to get to this point in my life. I am forever grateful to the teachers and mentors that helped make this life of poetry possible. Forever thankful to the kin who have been with me for as long as they've been with me, my ride or die homies. To all those who have shown me love. I would not be here without you. Especially thankful for Hannah Kezema; Raquel Salas Rivera; Tatiana Luboviski-Acosta; Erick Saenz; Farid Matuk; Raquel Gutiérrez; Carmen Giménez Smith; Anthony Cody; Josiah Luis Alderete; Vickie Vertiz; Angela Peñaredondo; Kit Schluter; Daniel Talamantes; Domingo Canizales III; MJ Malpiedi; Ariel Resnikoff; Elae Moss; Jackson Kroopf; DJ Jebejian; Alex Weinschenker; Felicia Rice; Kristen E. Nelson; Paul Ebenkamp; the entire Timeless, Infinite Light crew that first believed in *Black Lavender Milk*, Emji Saint Spero; Joel Gregory; Zoe Tuck; Gabriel Ojeda-Sagué; all my students from the CSUMB years; Ronaldo V. Wilson; CAConrad; Steve Dickison; Jamie Townsend; Ivy Johnson; Sesshu Foster; Andrea Rexilius; Anne Waldman; Eric Sneathen; Brent Armendinger; Elana Chavez; Kelan Daniels; Jack Goode; Josh Brodey;

my day ones David Barrios and Miles Johnson (shout out Van Nuys; shout out the gr818) and to everyone I forgot to mention or thank, know that I love you.

Eternally grateful to the bus drivers, service workers, pilots, and Taqueros who were there as I wrote some of these letters. Thanks to the editors that published previous versions of some of these letters in *The Berkeley Poetry Review*, *The Wanderer*, and especially to *Elderly Magazine* who published a collection of eight letters in 2016, first bringing Diego into the light.

Special thanks to the Nightboat crew, who so compassionately maneuvered through a pandemic and my own personal calamities to help shepherd this book into existence. *DESGRACIADO* could not have happened without Andrea Abi-Karam, Stephen Motika, Lindsey Boldt, Gia Gonzales, Caelan Nardone, and the entire Nightboat fam. It has been an absolute dream come true to work with you all. Thank you to my carnal, Kit Schluter for thinking, visioning, and working with me to imagine the cover you now hold in your hands.

Thank you to Farid Matuk and Susan Briante for holding space along the spine of the continent during Naropa University's Summer Writing Program all those years ago. That week continues to change my life and I remain forever grateful.

Thank you to Raquel Gutierrez, my Big Poppa, who took a chance on a chap that was not a chap, but in fact, a whole other path towards the future, way back when. EconoTextualObjects forever.

This book is secretly dedicated to mi rey, Raquel Salas Rivera, my ride or die. To the ancestors. To the future. To all kin who need it.

Thank you to everyone and everything that has ever tried to destroy me. I would have never found myself building this beautiful life without you. Thank you, Diego. Thank you, dear reader. May you live long enough to see your enemies fall.

xoxo,
A

ANGEL DOMINGUEZ

is a Latinx poet and artist of Yucatec Maya descent, born in Hollywood and raised in Van Nuys, CA by their immigrant family. They're the author of ROSESUNWATER (2021) and *Black Lavender Milk* (2015). Angel earned a BA from the University of California Santa Cruz and an MFA from the Jack Kerouac School of Disembodied Poetics at Naropa University in Boulder, Colorado. You can find Angel's work online and in print in various publications. You can find Angel in the redwoods or ocean.

NIGHTBOAT BOOKS

Nightboat Books, a nonprofit organization, seeks to develop audiences for writers whose work resists convention and transcends boundaries. We publish books rich with poignancy, intelligence, and risk. Please visit nightboat.org to learn about our titles and how you can support our future publications.

The following individuals have supported the publication of this book. We thank them for their generosity and commitment to the mission of Nightboat Books:

KAZIM ALI
ANONYMOUS (4)
ABRAHAM AVNISAN
JEAN C. BALLANTYNE
THE ROBERT C. BROOKS REVOCABLE TRUST
AMANDA GREENBERGER
RACHEL LITHGOW
ANNE MARIE MACARI
ELIZABETH MADANS
ELIZABETH MOTIKA
THOMAS SHARDLOW
BENJAMIN TAYLOR
JERRIE WHITFIELD & RICHARD MOTIKA

This book is made possible in part, by grants from the New York City Department of Cultural Affairs in partnership with the City Council, the New York State Council on the Arts Literature Program, and the Topanga Fund.